BRAVE
BOUNDARIES

Praise for *Brave Boundaries*

"Setting boundaries is a core skill of every successful leader. Every leader who wants to level up should read *Brave Boundaries!*"

—Cy Wakeman, *New York Times* bestselling author of *Life's Messy, Live Happy*

"Once again, Dr. Sasha Shillcutt finds the timeliest moment to bless us with her wisdom and inspire us to take control of our lives and happiness unapologetically and with courage."

—Dr. Sheila Nazarian, plastic surgeon, mom, entrepreneur, and Emmy-nominated Netflix star

"Dr. Sasha Shillcutt is a leading physician, clinical scientist, educator, author, speaker, phenomenal business woman, loving mother, and wife. She has the unique gift of giving you the permission you did not realize you needed to show up as your authentic self. In this book, she tells us how to break out of the bondage of societal expectations and set new brave boundaries to say no to commitments that steal our time and energy. This book is the unfiltered advice I needed to reclaim my time."

—Dr. Tiffany Love, PhD, APRN, FACHE, GNP, ANP-BC, CHC

"Dr. Sasha Shillcutt has written a brilliant how-to guide for the modern woman on how to say no without guilt. A must-have for any working woman!"

—Dr. Nneka Unachukwu, founder of the EntreMD Business School and host of the *EntreMD* podcast

"*Brave Boundaries* is a must-read for every woman! Sasha opens our eyes to where we need more boundaries and gives practical tools for creating a happier and healthier future."

—Alli Worthington, author and business coach

"Boundaries are critical for our mental health. Dr. Sasha Shillcutt takes the concept of boundaries and skillfully applies them to everyday life with liberating results. *Brave Boundaries* is a must-read for any leader striving for sustainable growth!"

—**Dr. Howard Y. Liu,** professor and chair, Department of Psychiatry, University of Nebraska Medical Center

BRAVE
BOUNDARIES

Strategies to Say No, Stand Strong, and Take Control of Your Time

The Key to Living Empowered

SASHA SHILLCUTT, MD

Health Communications, Inc.
Boca Raton, Florida

www.hcibooks.com

Also by Dr. Sasha Shillcutt

Between Grit and Grace
Health Communications, Inc.
1st edition (February 25, 2020)

**Library of Congress Cataloging-in-Publication Data
is available through the Library of Congress**

ISBN-13: 978-07573-2419-2 (Paperback)
ISBN-10: 07573-2419-3 (Paperback)
ISBN-13: 978-07573-2420-8 (ePub)
ISBN-10: 07573-2420-7 (ePub)

Publisher: Health Communications, Inc.
         301 Crawford Blvd., Suite 200
         Boca Raton, FL 33432-1653

Cover, interior design and formatting by Larissa Hise Henoch

To my fellow women physicians who, despite being underpaid, passed over for promotions, and excluded in places they belong, continue to show up day after day, saving lives and caring for "the least of these." May this book be a reminder that our worth is not defined by the limits or the value society has placed on us, and may you find the courage to set brave boundaries to live empowered.

Be who you are and say what you feel,
because those who mind don't matter,
and those who matter don't mind.[i]

—Bernard M. Baruch

CONTENTS

ACKNOWLEDGMENTS

This book wouldn't have been possible if I had not found myself in the pit of burnout at several times in my life when someone close to me said gently, "Sash, do you think you have taken on too much?" Ninety-nine percent of the time that person has been Lance Shill-cutt, who graciously picks up the pieces as he watches me learn the same lesson over and over; namely, that I must create and enforce boundaries for myself on a routine basis. The older I get, and the more success I find, the more I need radical, lifesaving boundaries.

Thank you to my best friend, Lance, who is kind enough to love the boundary-less Sasha, which is not a small feat. You are the greatest gift of my life God has blessed me with. Thank you to my children, Sam, Asher, Sophia, and Levi, who have borne the brunt of me learning life's greatest lessons. My hope for you is that, as you watch me set boundaries, you will be empowered to set your own.

Thank you to my parents and my sisters, who always encourage me to put out into the world what I believe I was made to share. Thank you to all my family members, who put up with me getting up at 5:00 AM, making coffee on vacation, and writing in between basketball games, on family vacations, and at dance practices. Thank you to my community, the women of The Table. You have stood by me as I navigated the most challenging year of my career, picking me up when I was knocked down. You followed me into the unknown, supporting me as I drew difficult and yet necessary lines in the sand. Your love and support are beyond what I deserve. You were with me in the dark places, and I am forever grateful for each of you who remained.

To my Brave Enough team—Chantel, Sarah, Jade—thank you for all your incredible patience with me. I am so blessed to have you in my life. Thank you for carrying the mission day to day and helping so many women thrive. To my circle: my sisters Leah, Michaela, Amy, Ali, Mina, Tara, Brittney, Steph, Jayme, Alli, Julie, Cy, Erica, AK, Aimee, and Dusty, thank you for not judging me but rather encouraging me to speak truth in the most unpopular areas.

To Dr. Gail Walling-Yanney, thank you for believing in me and giving me your wisdom to navigate the waters I find myself in.

To my amazing UNMC coworkers, truly, you are the best medicine has! Thank you for letting me be the weird one who challenges the status quo of academia.

To my boss and mentor, Dr. Steve Lisco, thank you for sponsoring, paying, and promoting so many women to lead. Your equity will be your legacy.

To the Old Widow Society and Rogue Enough, thank you for all the laughter, encouragement, and being secret holders. Save me a seat, I'm on my way.

Thank you to my agent Jeanne for your confidence in me and encouragement to cross the finish line.

To Christine, thank you for your excellent editorial guidance.

PREFACE

In 2013, I decided to pivot. I didn't decide to wake up out of some deep enlightenment on a beach or after hearing some phenomenal TED talk. I decided, out of necessity, to radically change how I approached my everyday life. I sat on the floor of my closet contemplating the reality that the life I was living was not the life I had envisioned for myself. I was burned out, emotionally depleted, physically exhausted, and empty. On paper, I was a successful up-and-coming cardiac anesthesiologist with four children under the age of seven. I looked good. On the inside, I was struggling to prove myself in the academic male-dominated world of medicine, crying myself to sleep each night when I would dare think of how bad I felt inside.

I was failing.

Over the course of a year, I made radical changes. I stepped into my power by owning the person God created me to be, by stepping out of everyone's expectations of me. I began by spending thirty minutes a day with myself. I started to prioritize my own well-being, my own wants and needs, saying "No" to the things others asked of me. I started peeling back the expectations of others by being okay with being unliked. I accepted being uncomfortable, as I moved from chronic people-pleaser to living life on my own terms. I centered my well-being. I prioritized my family over work. I became comfortable with the backlash that came with disappointing others who were used to me saying yes to everything and accepting unpaid work because I was a woman who should feel grateful that I was even considered for the task.

I set radical, lifesaving boundaries.

What came out of that year was more than me stepping into my power. I formed a sense of awareness about my own abilities and voice that I had never fully grasped prior. I felt courageous enough to start a community of women. What began with thirty women physicians, grew to nearly thirteen thousand, through my company, *Brave Enough*.

Over the past six years, I have learned through coaching and leading a community of thousands of high-achieving, educated women that the single most powerful weapon we possess to fight against overwhelm, exhaustion, and burnout is not what you think. It is not holding a specific degree, achieving a high-paying promotion, or bringing home a massive paycheck. It is not found in marrying the perfect mate or fitting into your college jeans. The key to living an empowered life is the ability to create and enforce radical, lifesaving boundaries—boundaries no one is teaching us, as women, to set.

Until now.

I have walked the typical, well-worn road professional women are told to run on the road to promotion. The way of people-pleasing, taking on extra and unpaid work, and doing the majority of domestic care and duties, all in the name of being a good mother, citizen, and team player. I have walked the path of career advancement that equates to operating at 150 percent capacity of your male peers, while making less pay, with promises to advance in due time. I have opened door after door required to make other people happy, both at work and at home, and lived the common experience of being told to be grateful for every opportunity given, even if that means being paid less or promoted more slowly.

I have grown wiser. I am no longer on that path.

I am qualified to write *Brave Boundaries*, because I have taught women at the highest level of leadership how to throw off the expectations of others and crush the patriarchal belief that we must be grateful for any crumb thrown our way for our talents and time. I wrote this book because I have coached hundreds of women on how to move from survival to thriving, all by embracing one key truth: *Only you can set boundaries in your personal and professional life.* No one is coming to clean up your life. No one is going to show up and suddenly remove tasks from your calendar and delete work you agreed to do for free from your to-do list. No one is going to give you permission to set boundaries. No one is coming.

Here's the good news: you do not need someone else to rescue you. You do not need a fairy godmother. You just need the knowledge, a little hutzpah, and a community. You will find all of those things here, in *Brave Boundaries*.

Stop looking over your shoulder, start looking forward.

Let's get to work.

INTRODUCTION

No matter how educated women are or how far they have climbed up the ladder, women are taught one thing over and over at every stage of their lives: *when someone asks you for help, you say "Yes."* Women are supposed to agree to take on whatever is asked of them, regardless of how busy they are or how much they have on their plate. No matter how much a woman deeply desires to say no, the societal expectation is that she say yes, because women are helpers.

We, as women, are taught to fix problems, always show up, and not let people down. We are instructed to never say no to tasks or duties asked of us, even when we are drowning in work and barely hanging on by a thread. When someone needs us, the expectation is that we will figure out how to make space for them.

When we become radically brave enough to say no, or we are so completely overwhelmed we can't take on another thing, we face backlash. It is uncomfortable and shocking. We dislike it. So, we often become avoiders. To avoid saying no, we hide. We conceal our talents or ideas, because we are too afraid someone will take advantage of them. We don't position ourselves in places of leadership, because we fear we will be taken advantage of and constantly be in service to others. When we do finally make it to a position of power and are in the spotlight, we find ourselves overperforming and overstretching ourselves to keep up the reputation of being a fiercely hardworking servant leader.

Our inability to say no, our avoidance, and our hiding often leads us to feelings of immense failure, inauthenticity, and burnout. Instead of recognizing our own power and control over our choices, we start to blame and shame ourselves. *What is wrong with me? Why do I not have the motivation to do more? Why do I not have the energy to take on more, to show up more?* These are the questions we ask ourselves. We label our ourselves as weak, saddle ourselves with guilt, and start the hopeless cycle of self-criticism.

I am going to tell you something radical: *Women do not need more motivation. We do not need fixing. We do not need more energy, a new and improved protein shake, or a new life coach. We do not need a special calendar app on our phone, a new nanny, or more Botox.*

We need boundaries: radical, lifesaving, abundantly clear boundaries. We need lines drawn around our priorities—fences that protect our physical health, our mental well-being, and provide opportunities for joy and growth. We need boundaries that say No to others and say Yes to ourselves. We need to set boundaries not only with our family and work colleagues but also with that one family member who calls and asks for advice at the most inopportune times. *Mostly, we need boundaries for our ourselves.*

We need clear, beautiful barriers around our time, our accessibility, our gifts, and our talents. We need to be able to say *No, thank you, I won't do that for free.* We need to stop lying and making excuses for why we can't show up for others and embrace the real truth and courageously share, *No, I cannot do that, because I am showing up for me.* We need to reset societal expectations of what a "kind" woman does, what a "hardworking" woman will and will not do, and what everyone expects us to be.

We need to take back the power of what we will do and where we will do it. We need to place ourselves in the driver's seat of our own time and be in control of our own work capacity. We are enough as we are. Radical, life-giving boundaries help us move from doormats and avoiders to empowered women. When we have strong boundaries, we make our own schedules, define our salaries, and create space for our own creativity, passion, and health.

As educated and empowered as we may be, society does not teach women to set boundaries. We may learn how to lead major companies, save lives, and teach armies of little people, but there's no class on how to become a boss lady who prioritizes her well-being by setting boundaries. I've taught thousands of women who own successful companies, lead academic departments, and have phenomenal skills in law, education, and technology, who find themselves completely empty, burned out, and miserable in their success. Over the last six years, I've coached everyone from Ivy League educated women to stay-at-home moms, and what I've learned is that, unless you understand how to set and enforce your personal boundaries, you will not find personal happiness.

Brave Boundaries is going to teach you how to identify breeches in your life boundaries and areas that need serious fences and take you through a personal boundary inventory. You'll learn how to change the way you approach your time management, get comfortable with the uncomfortable, and embrace saying *No* to others and *Yes* to yourself. You'll know how to respond to *boundary backlash,* recognize gender bias, and find peace in knowing it is okay to choose the healthiest you.

At the end of *Brave Boundaries,* you will be ready—ready for critical conversations with those who matter most to you. You'll be ready to take on that long-desired dream you've put on the back burner for years, waiting until there was enough time, because you will finally have more time for yourself. You will walk through life with a different mindset, and instead of avoiding people or responsibilities because you are so tired, you will see invitations to participate in things as compliments, not death sentences. You will realize that you are in control of what and who you allow into your life. You will be able to clearly determine what you should say yes to and what you should say no to, and you will gain peace.

I will show you how to set *Brave Boundaries* as I have done for thousands of women in my coaching classes and conferences. You will learn that boundaries are kind, not restrictive, and that being a person with boundaries is the most empowering and peaceful way to live.

Are you ready?

CHAPTER 1

SO VERY SMART, YET SO VERY TIRED

WHY DIDN'T I LEARN HOW TO
SET BOUNDARIES?

Every woman that finally figured out her worth,
has picked up her suitcases of pride and boarded a flight to freedom,
which landed in the valley of change.[ii]
—Shannon L. Alder, author

Walking to my boss's office, I find myself on the phone speaking in hushed tones to my son. "Calm down," I say in stern but barely audible tones. My phone vibrates. I pull it away from my ear and see my husband is calling on the other line. "I have to go," I tell my son. "Your father is trying to call me, and I have three minutes until I am due in my boss's office. I will discuss this with you when I am home."

I click the line over to my husband. In thirty seconds, he tells me about my son's angst. My son wants to drop a class, and he needs a decision pronto as the deadline is approaching. My husband, Lance, is busy at work and wants me to make the call. I deep breathe as I see I am approaching the door to my boss's office. "I CANNOT deal with this right now," I say in an exasperated voice. I hang up. I deep breathe. I steel my shoulders back and walk in.

"How are you?" I ask with a smile. Game face is on. I am present. I am here. I am prepared. Or am I?

As I sit down in my boss's office and begin to transition my thoughts to work, I am angry. I should not have answered the phone right before the meeting with my boss. Or maybe I should have? Perhaps I should have asked my boss to excuse me for five minutes and delayed the meeting. I could have called the school and taken care of my son's issue. Then, I could have texted my son, texted his father, and closed the loop. Now I am going to be thinking about this the entire time during the meeting.

Either way, I am disappointing someone I care about: my son or my boss. Why does it feel like, no matter how hard I try, I am constantly disappointing people? Then another thought invades my brain space: why does this problem fall on me right now? I understand why this is my problem, but why now? Why do I think I am the only one who can fix it? Why do I think I should be able to be both super parent and department leader at the same time? Would I ever expect this of one of my male colleagues? Would I have expected this of my female colleagues? If so, why?

HIDE YOUR CHEATING

The truth is this: we as women are expected to say Yes—Yes, every day, to every ask, to every need, to every responsibility. We are expected to show up, game face on, with immense love and capacity to help, fix, counsel, and please. It's like we are supposed to be part Marine, part Mary Poppins, and part Florence Nightingale. When someone needs us, day in or day out, we are to answer the call. We are to be there with a helping hand, a warm smile, and the knowledge of Yoda for whoever needs us, whether at work or home. And whatever we do, we are not to let one of our boyfriends know we are cheating on him; everyone has to be made to feel special. Our family, aka Boyfriend 1, otherwise known as Pete Personal, cannot possibly know that we are, in fact, seriously dating Boyfriend 2, aka William Work. And whatever you do, do NOT mention Pete Personal in front of William Work. This is a BIG no-no. I mean, even though everyone knows you are dating them both, you are pretty sure that if William Work acknowledged Pete Personal there would be cause for a massive blowup. So, we learn to navigate the art of dating them separately because, as women, it's taboo to talk about one in the presence of the other without backlash.

As women, we are constantly juggling both of our significant others. We are supposed to say yes to each of them whenever they call us or need us. Whether they are asking for a backrub or a spreadsheet does not matter. We are supposed to completely act as if we have it handled. We may find ourselves hanging out with Pete Personal when William Work calls, so we sneak out of the movie and answer the question. We may be in the middle of a major date night with William Work, and suddenly Pete Personal is having a crisis and needs some advice. We run to hidden hallways and sneak into bathrooms to take the call, then calmly return to William Work as if we were just powdering our noses. God help us. Truly. And we wonder why we find ourselves stuck in our cars in our garages having to will ourselves to transition from home to work and work to home. Have you ever driven home and thought, "How am I going to get out of the car? How am I going to go in there and help the people?" Bless it. All the people.

THE EXPECTATION OF YES

As professional women, we are trained that saying *no* is not an option, and when we are forced to say *no*, it's deeply uncomfortable. The backlash we know we will face for saying no leads us down a destructive path of over-functioning, where our own energy and capacity to function falls by the wayside with every step. We go through life increasing our capacity to help others over and over, until, like a balloon, we are so overstretched we explode. Our complete and utter exhaustion results in us being too tired to say no. It becomes easier to say yes even when we know we don't have the energy to do one more thing, and thus begets the cycle of overcommitment and overwhelm.

All kidding aside, the constant battle between the needs of those in our work life and those in our personal life leave us overworked and exhausted. Women find themselves empty and burned out, wondering why we are not more motivated, more energetic, or more capable of taking on more. It's like we are so used to just increasing our capacity to give, to do, to be more that we cannot accept the fact that there are limits to what we do, and that it is in our power to say no. We think there must be something wrong with us, because *why else would be so tired all the time?*

Aren't women smarter than this? According to the US Bureau of Labor Statistics, 29.5 million women in the US workforce have at least a bachelor's degree, compared to 29.3 million men in 2019.[iii]

Over the last three decades, women have made significant gains in education, entered the workforce in increasing numbers, and found themselves inching (albeit slowly) into top leadership positions. While equity in leadership still lags significantly and can be attributed to several different societal factors, an interesting conundrum exists—never have women reported more burnout or work dissatisfaction.[iv] If education and experience were all that was needed to achieve gender equity in the workforce, why doesn't the data reflect this? Why doesn't the data show that knowledge and experience are all women need to move forward and achieve job satisfaction? In fact, the opposite has been found. Women report more burnout, more workplace unhappiness, and decreased work-life balance than ever before.

After burning out in 2013, I wanted to hang up my stethoscope and quit medicine, a career at which I had worked ridiculously long and hard to attain. I dreamt of a job blindly folding yoga capris at Athleta. Sign me up. In my book, *Between Grit and Grace,* I share my story of overcoming burnout and rebuilding a life I did not want to escape from. It took me a good year to put myself back together, which started with making routine time for myself each day. But more than anything, the way I was able to maintain a busy career, motherhood, and start my own company, Brave Enough, without wanting to strangle every person I encountered, was dependent on one, important thing: my ability to set and protect radical, life-giving boundaries.

RADICAL BOUNDARIES: MY SAVIOR THEN AND NOW

What saved me in the darkest point of my life, and what has allowed me to thrive, was learning how to identify massive holes in the fence around my well-being. I learned how to commit to a life of self-preservation and that the only way I was going to have longevity and peace in balancing everything was if I became fiercely protective of my time and mental energy by placing strict boundaries. When I overcame burnout, found my passion in medicine again, and started to embrace my full and authentic self, I realized this important truth: the ONE change I made was not a career change, a partner change, or some life-gimmick—it was learning to see the cracks in the foundation of my well-being and seal them up with boundaries.

Setting these boundaries was not easy. They didn't always go well. At the beginning, I was so horrible at saying *no* that people laughed when I said it. No one took me seriously, and I had to say it many times. Everyone in my professional and personal life was so used to me saying *yes* to every crazy thing that I practically had to scream *NO* before people heard me. And when I did say *no* at the beginning of this journey to put my own sanity and health first, people used shame and blame to convince me to backtrack and regret saying it.

Once I recognized I needed radical boundaries, I started gaining the confidence to say no to others' expectations. I started seeing more clearly how other women around me were in the same situation. In the workplace, I constantly witnessed women colleagues exhausted from doing unpaid work and extra tasks they were assigned that they felt they must agree to in order to be taken seriously. I observed countless friends with full-time jobs doing 90 percent of the domestic work at home to be a "good mom," at the expense of their own health and well-being. And I thought to myself, *I have to change these inequities.* I knew that for women to take back control of their time and energy, we needed one another, and we needed radical change.

What came out of that dark period of my life was my company, *Brave Enough,* which I founded in 2017. What started as an online community in 2015, grew to an organization two years later when I saw the need for a company that supports the entire woman, both at home and at work. *Brave Enough* has become my life's mission, which is to teach women how to overcome burnout and set boundaries to take back control of their work and lives.

In 2017, I organized my first conference called the Brave Enough Women's Conference, which sold out the first day registration opened and crashed the server. The need for women to come together out of the community I had built was so evident to me that I then began to form small-group coaching sessions and classes. I started to reach women through a variety of ways: by starting my podcast *The Brave Enough Show,* speaking around the country on work-life challenges women face, and publishing research on gender inequity in the workplace. This work led me to reach thousands of high-achieving women through my courses, community, and conferences. And surprisingly, I found it did not matter if a woman was the chief operating officer of a health system, a teacher, or a nutritionist, there was common thread that was pervasive in women. Women were over-functioning and undervalued. Despite being brilliant, educated, and extremely hardworking, they lacked the one key ingredient to protect them from immense personal exhaustion. They did not know how to identify much-needed personal boundaries, they lacked knowing how to say no, and they were not sure how to stand strong in the face of what I call *boundary backlash.*

NO? SAY WHAT?

It is not that thousands of brilliant, hardworking, educated women were not smart enough or strong enough. We are both these things. Rather, it is that setting boundaries and the ability to say *No, thank you,* without facing harsh criticism, feedback, or labeling is not something women are offered in our society. Everyone, even the most well-meaning colleagues, safe work environments, and loving family members, expects women to say *yes*—over and over. Trust me, this is not some far-reaching feminist propaganda. This is the blatant truth: society does not know how to respond to a woman who says *no* without apology. We are so used to women saying yes that we ask women every day to work for free, or even ask them to pay to work and, as a society, we think nothing of it. Because this is the expectation of women, most women say yes, and the gender pay gap widens a little bit more.

FACT: Our world runs on the backs of women with zero boundaries.

Our society is constructed for women to keep doing more for less. Our entire social structure depends on women opening their arms to take on more tasks, carry one more responsibility until the balls begin to drop, and then figure out how to reach down and pick up even more duties. When we are so overburdened that we have to relinquish some responsibilities or people, instead of asking for help or saying, *I cannot carry you anymore,* women are taught to instead look at themselves in the mirror and ask, "What is wrong with me? I should be stronger." We find ourselves apologizing for our inability to do it all, start searching the internet for a magic pill that will give us more energy, or think to ourselves we need more education, a different workout routine, or a new skincare regimen.

In my coaching classes, I have coached hundreds of highly successful women who are completely burned out and desperate for change. They know they need to change, but they aren't sure where to begin. What is most fascinating is that, 99 percent of the time, they come into the class with the false belief that they are weak, inept, and lack something.

"Tell me about your typical work week," I'll say to one client. "Well, I worked an overnight shift from 5:00 PM to 7:00 AM. I got home around 9:00 AM after finishing up some charting. My son was sick, so I spent some time taking him to the doctor in the morning, and then the nanny came, so I could sleep for a few hours," my client, an emergency medicine physician and mother of two young boys, tells me. "I woke up a few hours later, did some laundry, made dinner for my family, and then went back for another night of work in the emergency department. But don't worry, next week I will have more time to get things done. I just can't seem to figure out why I am too tired to work on my research or redo the curriculum I need to get to. Can you help? Something is definitely wrong with me. I should have more energy," she says. Sound familiar?

What has struck me is that rarely have I ever coached a woman who has told me they need help creating boundaries, saying no, and negotiating for more time or money to accomplish all of the things they are continually expected to do for free. But over and over, women ask me to help them find more energy, more capacity, and more ability to "do." Women do not see their burden of work as an insurmountable task they cannot achieve without self-destruction, but rather, they see themselves as the problem, as they are convinced that they are just not enough.

IMPERFECT? PERFECT!

Women do not need to be more energetic, stronger, or more anything. They need to be offered the ability to say *no,* free of backlash.

They need to be offered pay for jobs, roles, and tasks they are asked to take on and not have to negotiate for the same pay offered to their male colleagues for the same jobs. Women need to be afforded help when it is needed, offered opportunities that result in more work-life control, and allowed to say no without the fear of backlash, retaliation, or shame. We need a societal reset in the expectations of what a working woman looks like. She should not look tired, exhausted, overworked, and undervalued.

And that starts with boundaries—radical, lifesaving boundaries. As much as we would love for people in our professional and personal lives to understand and respect our limits, we can't. The world operates on a playing field of expecting women to say *yes,* so saying *no* is not something we learned as girls, teenagers, young women, or early career women. No one teaches us it is okay to say no even if we face backlash: not our teachers, our mentors, our sponsors, our bosses, our family, or our spouses. This is something I had to learn on my own, and I promise you, if I can do it, so can you.

I want you to think of *Brave Boundaries* as a weapon. In this book, you will learn powerful tools you can use to recreate a life according to your values, your priorities, and your well-being. You will learn to identify common thought distortions that often make us think we do not have control over our lives and decisions. Through the next several chapters, you will see that you do not need to be more of anything; you are enough as you are. What you need is to place a fence. You need to start with fence posts, and the muscles you grow as you start to dig holes will only make you stronger. Each post will get easier to lift and place in its hole. Each post will be a reminder that you are erecting a fence, protecting your health, and you are strong enough to get it done.

You will learn to review your life section by section and take inventory of where gaps exist. You will see what areas of your life are burning you out, what you want more of, and what you need less of. You will see spaces of your life that are wide open pastures with no fences, and thus the animals run wild and have stripped the fields of much-needed nutrients. You will see sections of your life that are completely barren because you have never watered them. You will see where you have never said *no* to the people who take and take and take from you, and you somehow blamed yourself for that. You will see how much of yourself you have lost from years of saying *yes* to everyone else and *no* to yourself.

Your journey through *Brave Boundaries* will not be easy. It will likely take you into spaces of grief where you are sad for the parts of yourself you have lost along the way. You will realize there are people, places, and organizations that you thought appreciated all the time you gave them who, in truth, likely appreciated the work you did for them, but not you. You will see areas of your life where the fear of letting others down or the fear of a backlash led you to say yes over and over. You will see how, despite being strong in some areas of your life, you may be paralyzed with fear in other spaces that you are too afraid to address.

FACT: You do not have to feel strong or ready to create brave boundaries.

That is okay. That is the purpose of *Brave Boundaries*. You do not have to be perfect to start this book. You do not have to have perfect boundaries, have the perfect life, or be the strongest version of yourself before you continue the work here. You do not need to be MORE of anything other than what you are—perfectly imperfectly you. Every single one of us has spaces in our lives around which the thought of placing boundaries scares us beyond measure, while we find other areas are as easy to protect as Fort Knox.

The challenge with boundaries is that they are highly specific to each of us according to our pasts, our personalities, our position in our families of origin, and our current home and work environments. But we cannot let that stop us from doing the hard work of investigating our boundaries (or lack thereof) by digging deep. We are women, and we do hard things.

CELEBRATE THE NO WOMAN

Once we realize that women setting and enforcing boundaries is abnormal for our society and that we have never been taught to do this as part of our education or training, we begin to take a deep breath and accept that it is natural that both feel uncomfortable and unknown. We can remove the pressure that, somehow, we aren't strong enough to have figured this out ourselves or that we are the type of women who aren't made for boundaries. Frankly, I am so over the Instagram-worthy Pinterest-perfect version of what women are supposed to be. The reason we need boundaries is because we do not celebrate women who say no, thank you, in the first place. We love women who look like they have it all, bring home the bacon, and look good doing it. We love women who get along with everyone because they never disappoint anyone by saying no. We love women who say yes, *I can do that!* And we frown on women who say nope, no way, and a big fat nada. It's true. Our society loves yes women.

Let me give you some tough love and some much-needed grace at the same time. We, as yes women, are drowning. With every yes, we let another person into the already cramped space of our lives, and, as a result, a small piece of ourselves walks out the back door.

We become Grade A people-pleasers and lose so much of our own identity that we do not even know who we are anymore. When we finally come to a full stop, it is not to say *what you are expecting of me is not healthy for me to do,* but is often because we think, *gosh, I can't keep up, something must be wrong with me.* We lose our own ability to see that we are MORE than yes women, that we are more than what we can do or give to others, that we are unique individuals with ideas and passions, who are meant to be cultivated and shared with the world. The problem is, we find it easier to say yes to others' ideas for us than yes to our own ideas. And when we do say yes to ourselves, we are labeled as selfish, difficult, or not the team players we are supposed to be.

One of the most difficult and vital things we do as women is to draw those first, strong lines in the sand; to go against the grain of what we are expected to be, of what we often have been for so long; to reset the lines that have never existed around our work, our home and family life, and our personal goals. It is both scary and awkward but at the same time incredibly freeing and empowering.

YES MOM

I will never forget one of the scariest boundaries I set with my best friend, who also happens to be my husband, Lance. We often think the easiest boundaries we set will be those that involve people who understand us and know us best. But I have found in my own life, and in coaching hundreds of women, that the opposite is true.

In 2013, I was completely burned out. I was a busy anesthesiologist trying to climb the ladder in academia, with four tiny people at home who needed me 24/7. Despite trying everything I could to be all things at both home and work, I was failing everywhere. I saw no way out of my overwhelmed, exhausted, and overcommitted life. When I finally got to the tipping point, which I describe in my first book, *Between Grit and Grace,* I was an engine running full blast forward on the hot mess express.

I knew something had to change and that it had to start with me spending time alone with myself on a routine basis. The truth is, I was terrified to spend time alone. When the inside of your brain looks like a pantry that's been ransacked by monkeys, you do NOT want to go in there. You want to run in, get what you need as fast as you can, and run out. But I knew the dumpster fire that was my mind was not going to reorganize itself. And it started with time alone.

The problem was my family was used to me as Yes Mom. *Yes Mom* was this superwoman who did everything for everyone. Yes Mom cleaned the house, cooked, went through all the school papers each night, emptied the dishwasher before bed, and changed out the laundry after putting the kids to bed. While her husband was working out each night, Yes Mom ran around like a crazy woman so the following day could happen without something falling in the cracks.

As Yes Mom, I was empty. I was completely worn out, and I knew I had to make a change. I knew I had to start getting up an hour earlier and spending time on my own self-care. But as an anesthesiologist who works insane hours, to get up an hour earlier, I had to go to bed an hour earlier. Who was going to do all the things I did for an hour before bed? I knew if I didn't do them, they would not get done. They would not get done unless my husband gave up working out each night, which I did not want to ask him to give up. I did not want extra stress in our marriage, which was already strained with two full-time working parents, four kids, and an unruly dog that chewed a ridiculous amount of furniture. Wasn't I supposed to support my husband and make sure he was taken care of, just like I took care of my patients and my kids? I knew if I told my husband I wasn't going to do all the things each night that literally had to be done or the train would derail, he would do them. He would take over and help me, but I also knew his only opportunity to work out was after the kids were in bed. I knew he would be mad inside, angry at me, and bitter. I would have let him down.

The problem was that I had to discuss this with him, no matter how scary or how much I felt like I was disappointing him. You would think I would be able to set this boundary with the person who saw me mid labor screaming at nurses in my pre-epidural state. But instead, I just avoided the conversation and the topic with him big-time. I then made up my mind that I was going to bed an hour earlier, but I wasn't going to tell him. I was just going to do it and see what happened. Maybe it would all be fine. Maybe a bedtime-clean-the-kitchen fairy would appear and go through the school papers, and finish the laundry, and start the dishwasher each night. Maybe he wouldn't notice my absence, and things could just keep going on. Right?

EWWW, BACKLASH

Guess what happened? My boundary had a ripple effect on the entire family. It did not go unnoticed, and it required significant explanations and crisis management. There may have been some raised voices. Actually, there *were* raised voices. There was conflict. My boundary, albeit healthy for me, derailed the family train. The papers piled up. The dishes weren't clean. My husband stopped working out during his hour to do all the things I had done. Over the next three months, he grew irritable and bitter. I avoided the conversation, the most important one, of why I needed this boundary. I didn't give him enough credit, and I thought he wouldn't understand. But the opposite was true. My husband wanted me to thrive. He wanted me to come out of the burned-out state and have energy to participate in family fun again. The truth was that my fear wasn't in setting the boundary, my fear was the backlash I thought I would experience once I set it.

I was wrong. Yes, there was backlash. But the backlash was because I did not explain what I was doing or why. I just did it. I just set the boundary and expected everyone in my family to get the "new" me. Once the train was derailed, and our family suffered some serious bumps over the next several months, I had to explain the *why* of what I was doing. And once I did, my husband not only understood and respected my boundary, he met me in the middle. It didn't take long, in fact, he was supportive immediately. We figured out we needed to hire someone to come in the morning and help us out. With help, I could work out in the mornings. He could work out at night. It took us a few months, but eventually, we got there. The family train was back on the rails. We respected one another's boundaries, and the stuff of life got done.

Looking back, it seems silly to me that a full-fledged professor, cardiac anesthesiologist, and gender-equity researcher was afraid to tell her husband she was changing her bedtime hour. I am the person who has zero problems setting boundaries for my patients and will go toe to toe with anyone to protect them. Feel free to laugh at the hilarity of me NOT wanting to go toe to toe with my husband over the dishwasher. But it's true; I avoided the conversation with my husband at all costs. Like many women, I was tired. I was too tired to face the backlash I perceived would happen as a result of setting a boundary.

Backlash is real. Not every boundary we set is with our best friend who understands and respects us. Sometimes, the boundaries we as women set result in significant anger, social isolation, or even loss of a job or role. Some boundaries are not with others, but they are limitations, promises, and oaths we must make with ourselves. Those are often the hardest ones to make, where the only person who knows if we are keeping the boundary is ourself.

FACT: Just because someone loves you does not mean they will love your boundaries.

Over the next several chapters, we are going to learn that our biggest challenge in life is not finding the right mojo or motivation; it isn't finding the right person or job or new bestie that is going to make us less tired, feel more in control, or less overwhelmed. The key is in our ability to set boundaries, keep promises to ourselves, and show up for our own priorities. You will learn to develop your inner leader and identify areas of your life where you have zero boundaries. You will be empowered to properly say no to asks and needs from others that conflict with your well-being and priorities. You will see how you have avoided certain people or places simply because you are afraid of the backlash of saying no. You will learn how to overcome the overwhelm and fatigue by standing strong in the decisions you make for your own health. You will find the strong you, who is not afraid to set boundaries and who does not fear the backlash that often comes with enforcing them.

You ready?

Boundary Check-In

1. As you start to think about boundaries in your life, think about your biggest pain point. Yes, go there. Breathe. You got this.

2. What area of your life causes you the most strife? Is it a person, a work project, a family member, or a personal issue that you just can't seem to overcome? Is it someone or something you are desperate to avoid?

3. Your largest pain point in life likely is either a person, a problem, or a project in which you have the least boundaries. Your pain point is one, I would hedge to bet, where you either fear setting boundaries, are not sure how to set them, or feel boundaries would be completely impossible as the task or relationship is on your "required," non-negotiable list.

4. As we move through the next several chapters, it will be important to have that pain point in your view. You will use it as your guide to learn to create boundaries. If you're not sure what it is, don't worry. Below is an exercise that will help you define it.

YOUR PRIORITIES VERSUS YOUR PAIN POINTS: AN EXERCISE

In my life, I have found that at any given time I have room for three top priorities. Yes. That is it. I truly only have the time and energy for three other focuses, projects, or people. Now, these things change year to year, and that is the beauty of living a dynamic life. When coaching women in my Brave Balance master class, I often use the following analogy to demonstrate this: for the rest of your life, you are driving a four-seater car. There is only room in your car for four people. You are in the driver's seat. There is room in your car for your family (and friends who are family) in one seat, perhaps your career is in another seat, which leaves one seat open for a hobby, a passion, a community, or whatever you chose to focus on this year.

Just like any car, you can let more people and projects into your four-seater than you have seatbelts for. But the ride won't be comfortable, and you will feel confined, uncomfortable, and at times like you can't even see to drive. The more priorities you let in as time goes on, because you don't get a bigger car, you just become more cramped. The ride becomes stressful, weighted down, and cumbersome. Once you realize this, you can be extremely careful to stop and ask yourself before letting in any other passengers: does this person, task, or project deserve the fourth seat?

Let's do a quick exercise to define your priorities. Each January and July I do this exercise. I write down my three "passengers," or priorities, for the year. I used to do it once a year, but now I have found my priorities can change over the year, and that the freedom to change them is empowering. Defining these priorities will allow you to focus on what boundaries you need in your life as we go through *Brave Boundaries,* with the result being that you have defined your pain points.

1. Grab a journal and make a square with four quadrants. In one quadrant, write YOU. Ask yourself, in the next year, how do I want to invest in myself? Maybe it is taking an online class. Maybe it is taking that girls' trip you've always wanted to go on. Maybe it is making a commitment to yourself to do a daily meditation or prayer. In one to three bullets, list how you are going to show up for yourself this year. Be realistic and kind to yourself. Investing in yourself should means finding ways you are honoring yourself as a woman. For example, this year,

mine says, "Take a daily destress walk." A decade ago, it would
have read, "Lose ten pounds." But truly, my daily walk is much
healthier for me than being a certain jean size, and it is more
attainable. So, this is one of my bullet points under "You."

2. Now move on to the next quadrant. Only you get to decide
   what priorities you write in your quadrants. Maybe one is
   your family. Ask yourself, what it is that you'd like to achieve
   this year with your family? For me, one bullet point is a daily
   check-in with my kids: a touch point to see how they are,
   maybe a hug, a text. You may think that isn't much but, as a
   full-time physician mom of four, this is a huge goal for me.
   Yours may be a vacation you want to take, or perhaps a relationship you want to repair.

3. Perhaps the next quadrant is your career, or your passion,
   side-hustle, or promotion you are working for. Perhaps it is
   running that half-marathon you've always wanted to do. There
   are no right or wrong answers here! Take time to contemplate
   this question: if I had all the time in the world, what would
   I focus on? Who would the other three "passengers" be? For
   example, in my three other quadrants for this year, there is my
   family, my work, and writing this book. That is all I had time
   for this year. This was not the year I could take on training
   for a marathon, publishing research, or taking on speaking
   engagements. It is extremely important to have these priorities, because as you are asked to take on other passengers, it
   allows you to say, *no, I am sorry, this ride is full.*

4. Now, find a sticky note and write out your three other priorities. Place the sticky note on your bathroom mirror. Write

them on another note and place it on your calendar or planner. Each day, when you open your calendar, have those priorities in view. Another idea is to create an image of these three priorities as your phone screen saver and your computer background. Place them where you access them daily so that you are reminded of what they are. My sticky notes have a bullet or two under each one to remind myself of what I am focusing on. *These are your priorities.*

5. The final step is to write out who is actually in your car right now. Chances are, there are many other passengers who do not belong there. Why are they there? Has someone told you it's your responsibility to drive them? Are they there out of guilt, unseen pressure, or fear of backlash? Which passengers do you want to stop and ask to exit? Which ones are you holding on to because you actually like them but aren't sure you have the capacity to keep driving them around?

6. These extra passengers are likely related to your biggest pain points in life. Sometimes, it is a project at work you said yes to and don't see an exit strategy. It may be a person who doesn't respect your boundaries and emotionally drains you. It may be a past failure you can't seem to let go of. Instead of processing and letting go, you have invited it into your vehicle year after year and are constantly asking yourself, *why does the journey feel so heavy?*

This exercise may seem extreme. You may be thinking, *but Sasha, you definitely focus on more than three other priorities a year!* You are right. There are times I find myself focusing on more than three in addition to my own self-investment. However, 99 percent of the time when this happens, a month doesn't pass before I am wiped out, exhausted, and my top three priorities start to suffer. Most of the time it is because I have failed to keep strong boundaries around the other passengers and have said yes to tasks that do not fit in one of the three quadrants.

They key to living our priorities is to remove passengers five, six, seven, and eight. Do everything in your power to keep only three other passengers in your car at any given time. You may swap them in and out, but you decide to only allow three others in.

Now that you have defined them, BREATHE. Remember, you are in the driver's seat. You may feel like you have been in the passenger seat, but as we walk through *Brave Boundaries,* the journey will show that you are in control.

CHAPTER 2

BOUNDARIES? YUCK.

DEFINING BOUNDARIES AND THE DIFFERENCE BETWEEN PROFESSIONAL AND PERSONAL BOUNDARIES

We expect women to work like they don't have children,
and raise children as if they don't work.

—Amy Westervelt, *Forget Having It All*

For the last five years, I have spent countless hours with high-achieving, highly educated, powerful women. These women work in all types of industries: education, healthcare, law, and technology. They're brilliant executives, lawyers, entrepreneurs, founders, influencers, and leaders. But despite having career expertise, subject knowledge, and life experience that is quite frankly extraordinary, they are missing something critical: professional success without sacrificing personal well-being.

I meet these women at my conferences and hang out with them at my retreats. I spend hours in classes with them and read their e-mails where they describe the same thing over and over: they are burned out, feel like they are failing to keep up, and, mostly, are emotionally and physically exhausted. Here is the thing that is really mind blowing: *they have been convinced by our society it is their fault they cannot do it all and look good while doing it.*

WHAT IS WRONG WITH YOU?

Yep, that is correct. The women I coach believe they just haven't found the special sauce yet, and that is why they are struggling with finding any sense of personal well-being. If they could only be a little more like the men, they would be okay. If they could just be stronger, care less for their children, ignore their neighbors, and not worry about their aging parents, they'd be able to handle it all. If they could just stop doing all the things that need to be done around the house and get on the spin bike, they'd find "balance." If they could ignore the dishes (I mean, SOMEONE will do them eventually, right?) and not worry about school papers piling up, they'd feel rested! Who cares about feeding the family? Can't they feed themselves? These women are told they just need better time management, more meditation, and less empathy. Then, they will feel better, sleep better, have less stress, and move up the ladder faster! Come on, girls! You can do it!

SCREECHING HALT, *RECORD SCRATCHING NOISE* I CALL FOUL!

Imagine that I am standing in front of you with my hands on my hips, calling a big, old-fashioned timeout. No, no, and no. One of the first things I teach women, after taking a burnout assessment is that there is nothing wrong with you. You do not need to be more like a man. You are not a man. The reason you are exhausted and have no time for yourself is because you are not meant to do the work of ten people. You are meant to do the work of one. You are simply, yet dangerously, overcommitted. You are over-functioning. You need ONE radical, life-changing intervention: to implement, and stand by, your personal boundaries.

FACT: There is nothing wrong with you. You are exhausted because you are overcommitted.

I am probably going to make a few enemies here, but the truth is, men are not required in our society to set the same number of boundaries women are. Why? Because they do not have the same assumed responsibilities that we women do. They do not have the same societal expectations to be caregivers, domestic managers, or emotional nurturers. I recognize I am speaking in gender generalities here, but society does not place the same expectations on working men as it does on working women. A second important difference is that, when men set boundaries, they are respected; when women set boundaries, they are rejected.

When men set boundaries, they are respected; when women set boundaries, they are rejected.

For many years, I would notice in the workplace women doing an enormous amount of work that someone had to do but didn't really "count" for career advancement. In other words, the work assigned to women had to be done to keep the cylinders firing and the machine moving forward, but at the end of the year, these tasks didn't result in a larger paycheck or something women could list on a resume for a promotion. I remember my senior year of anesthesia residency, as I was about to graduate, my chairman gave me a solid piece of career advice. "If you want to be successful in academia, you need to be selfish," he told me one day as I sat across from him in his office. I asked him what he meant by selfish, and he further explained: "Do not accept roles that won't get you ahead. Do not do things that don't result in pay or promotion. Follow the men," he stated.

FOLLOW THE MEN

I can't tell you how many times I have thought of his words. Like it or not, he was telling me the truth. He was advising me to not fall into the trap of doing tasks that most of the time were given to women in our department, that cost time and energy, but came with no pay or leadership resulting from the womanpower put in. The truth is, I was truly thankful for his advice at the time. I recognized that he wanted me to be successful, a leader, and he was sharing a secret truth with me: women are given tasks and titles that result in work and hours but come without pay or promotion. I was going to avoid those! I would be like the guys. I was going to get ahead.

Now, a decade and a half later, when I think of his advice, it incites anger. Why are women given those tasks? Furthermore, why is ANYONE? Why are women expected to do work that keeps the machine rolling forward, while men are given roles and work that is more likely to result in pay, promotion, and power? The sad truth is that many organizations and companies run on the backs of women who are afraid to say no and set boundaries when they are asked to do such tasks. In 2019, I set out to dive deeper into this issue and conducted a research study. Tired of hearing "those are just anecdotes, Sasha," I wanted to prove what I knew was true.

CITIZENSHIP TASKS

In 2020, we published our research in the *Journal of Women's Health,* showing that women report doing more citizenship tasks, or unpaid work in the workplace, than their male counterparts.[vi] Not only are women doing unpaid work at home, they are also more likely than men to be expected to take on work in their organizations that requires significant time and skill but does not result in pay or promotion. This research confirmed what I was hearing from the countless women I coached: women need boundaries now more than ever to remain in the workplace, get paid for the work they do, and find the voice to say no to work that does not pay or promote them.

And if you think it is bad for all of us women, the expectations placed on minority women in the workplace are even more taxing. Under-represented minority women are often asked to go the extra mile for anyone and everything needing to be done in the workplace. As my friend Dr. Sheritta Strong, Assistant Vice-Chancellor of Inclusion at the University of Nebraska Medical Center, and award-winning psychiatrist, once told me when describing the expectations of minority women in the workplace, "Sasha, we are invisible at the same time we are on a display. All eyes are on us." In their article in the *Journal of Women's Health,* Rodriguez and colleagues described the common thread under-represented minority women experience in the workplace, as they are often asked to take on even more unpaid additional citizenship tasks than their white female counterparts.[vii] Minority women are expected to agree to do extra work willingly, while also facing systemic racism in their daily work environment. It is beyond exhausting, and the backlash they may face for setting and enforcing boundaries layers additional stress on their work lives and personal well-being.

FACT: Women are asked to do more tasks that do not result in pay or promotion in their workplaces than are men.

SECOND-SHIFT EFFECT

Never before has the need for lifesaving boundaries been more critical. According to the McKinsey Report, "Women in the Workplace," published in September 2020, the COVID-19 pandemic has set back women in the workplace more than a half a decade.[viii] One in four women in the United States are contemplating leaving the workforce due to the pressure of the "second shift."[ix, x] The second shift is commonly referred to as what working women are faced with after finishing their workday, where data shows that regardless of work status, professional women report doing several more hours of domestic and childcare duties than men in similar occupations each week. One study done by Jolly and colleagues, published in the *Annals of Internal Medicine* on early career physicians, found that woman physicians reported working 8.5 hours more each week on domestic and childcare duties than age- and rank-matched male physicians of similar occupation and full-time employee status.[xi]

The immense pressure on women to work both shifts—their

careers and their homes—coupled with the immense responsibility women have faced during the pandemic to virtually teach their children with less childcare support, has resulted women having to choose between their careers or the health of their families. Men have not reported similar rates, leaving the harsh reality that women are leaving the workforce in droves, setting back gender equity, and the much-needed growth of women into leadership positions, like we have not seen. Learning how to develop and implement brave boundaries is needed more than ever. It is not just at work you need to find your voice to say *no*. In Chapter 2, beyond recognizing your strength and power in the workplace, we are going to identify the need to set clear boundaries around paid- and unpaid-work expectations in the workforce *and at home.*

FACT: We need fierce boundaries in our homes, not just our workplaces.

YOU CAN DO ANYTHING! BUT ALSO . . .

The truth is that there is a very real expectation placed on women to be the domestic goddesses of their homes. And let me stop you right there if you think that this only applies to women who are mothers or who care for children in their home. It is true for all women I know, whether they are married, single, divorced, with or without children.

We are born as women into a world that hangs a large sign out front that says women can be anything, do anything, and achieve anything we set our hearts on doing. All we need is a little luck, a solid education, and a work ethic . . . right? Want to be the CEO of a company someday? It is yours. A doctor? You got it! A lawyer? You can! Want to create art or music or own your own small business? Just dream it. You can be it. Want to have a successful career AND a blossoming family? You got it!

But the truth is this: there is a BUT. There is a clause that is hidden behind every dream we have. Behind each decision we make, each opportunity we weigh heavily on our minds, we find ourselves pausing to examine the cost. Because hanging on to the end of every contract, every promotion, every opportunity we are presented with is a fine print clause that is NOT in the same contract for the majority of men. We have an addendum as women, a tiny put powerful add-on to each opportunity that presents itself that reads: *You can do this, but remember what else you are signed up to do this week. You have to keep the house afloat: keep the fridge stocked, clean up after the humans, check in with your family members, change out the laundry between business calls, and make sure the school papers have been organized.*

You may be reading this and think it sounds completely archaic, paternalistic, and straight outta 1965. You would be right. It is.

The truth is that while we as women have made significant gains in our education, in career opportunities, and in our professional advancement in the last forty years, *we did not set down the domestic expectations that come with being a woman.* We just kept carrying them; not because we wanted to, but because everyone, and I mean everyone, expects us to. We never stopped being "in charge" of our home life, of caring for our children, of making sure someone feeds the dog. While many of us have amazing partners who share the burden, the truth is that the majority of us are still considered the chief operating officer of our domestic and childcare duties. And before you start to question this truth, I challenge you to ask yourself the following questions. Whether you are a woman or man, these questions may reveal some truths in your home life and the way you "see" your role in your partnership or relationships. Be open minded, be brave, and be honest with yourself as you ask these questions.

- Who delegates household duties in your home?

- Do you have to "ask" for help, or is it assumed you are no more responsible for figuring out how your children will get from point A to point B than your partner or spouse?

- Do others in your family—for example, your own parents or in-laws—have expectations of you as a woman (or the woman in your life) to make sure certain domestic duties are being done?

- How comfortable are you asking for help for domestic or childcare duties? Do you struggle with feelings of guilt when you hire someone to help you with these tasks or when you ask a neighbor or friend to help you with childcare?

- When you have to attend a work event, stay late at night, or leave for work travel, who organizes the household duties that must be done in your absence? Do you share these organizational assignments with your partner, or does it fall solely to one or the both of you?

- If you are single and in a relationship, do you find yourself doing household duties for your partner, even if you do not share a living space?

IN CHARGE OF EVERYTHING (PLUS SOME)

I consider myself a woman who knows how to ask for help and does so often. The truth is, I could never accomplish all that I do without help from my husband, family, friends, coworkers, employees, and neighbors. There would be no *Brave Enough* company. There would be no conferences, courses, or books. It takes a village to do this mission, and it also takes a village to raise my children with any semblance of organization. Despite having a ton of help and resources, I found myself in the middle of the pandemic in 2020 really struggling to manage all things. I am a big proponent of seeking mental health for yourself and erasing the stigma of therapy. For the first time in a decade, I found myself needing to talk to someone who could help me process some deep feelings of inadequacy and failure I was struggling to process.

In our first meeting, the therapist asked me to describe my current support system. I jumped right in and starting bragging about my awesome husband. I told her how he "helps me at home a ton. He helps me run the kids to and fro. He helps them get to all their sporting and school stuff in an organized manner. He helps me drive them all over. And when I travel for work, he helps manage them day to day and does a great job. He is a huge help to me."

She smiled back and me, set down her glasses and said, "Do you realize what you just did? You said: *'he helps me.'*"

I stared at her, confused. I mean, I know I am biased, but Lance Shillcutt is an amazing dad. He is the bomb-diggity. You cannot find a better dad than my husband. I will fight you over these words. They are true.

My therapist went on and revealed something deep in my subconsciousness that I did not even realize I had been holding on to—a narrative I had created for myself and clung to that created a lot of guilt and anxiety. She revealed the fine print. She revealed the addendum. "You are placing yourself as the main person responsible for your entire household and your children. You are referring to your husband taking care of your kids as 'helping you.' You are referring to him doing things that need to be done in your absence as 'helping you.' You have listed all the ways he helps you, as if you are the responsible person, and he is your helper."

I took a deep breath and fought back tears. She was right. The truth is my husband *did* help me. That was not the issue. The issue was that I believed that all of the house duties, childcare duties, and other domestic life tasks *belonged to me*. They were listed in my job description as a wife and a mother. And if I wanted to excel as a wife and a mother, if I wanted to reach full professorship and even tenure, I had better take full responsibility and delegate those tasks I could not do. Despite having a full-time job as a physician and running a business, I was carrying the weight of the ultimate responsibility for those under my roof and even in the roof itself.

The problem with this is that when you view your family, your home, and others as your primary responsibility, and not one that is shared if you are in a partnership, several things happen. First, you fail, because you cannot do all these things, nor are you meant to. Things slip through the cracks. The second is that bitterness sets in. You start to become angry and resentful that you alone are responsible for delegating all the tasks in your domestic space. You wonder why you have to do it all and at the same time hold close the fact that you must do it all. Third, your ego grows. You become addicted to the idea that only you can really run things right—remember to buy the light bulbs for the basement and order the perfect birthday cake. While you are running on fumes, you are also dangerously feeding your ego. The world loves the super woman who never says *no,* handles it all, and brings home the bacon, and you soak it up.

Finally, there comes the guilt. Because you physically and mentally cannot do it all, you have to ask for help. But your ego tells you this is a bad thing, so you feel guilty. You feel guilty asking your neighbor to carpool with your kids. You feel guilty your spouse had to cook dinner every night this week while you were at working late on a deadline. Or perhaps you are a single parent, and you feel guilt about it all. You should be able to handle all of this, right?

Um, no. Dear Lord, *no.*

FACT: When you own the primary responsibility for all domestic or child-rearing duties, you are carrying a burden too great to bear alone.

IF NOT ME, WHO?

You may be reading this and thinking, *Oh yeah? But if not me, then who?* I understand not everyone has the same resources, a family or community support system, or a partner. But we must remove the false belief that we, as women, must own the primary responsibility of all domestic or parenting duties, and we must remove the stigma that asking for help equals failing as women. And the most important distinction is this: *You may not think you should do it all, but you still may be holding onto the belief that as a woman, you must delegate it all. In other words, you are ultimately in charge of all domestic and child-rearing duties, and the buck stops with you.*

This is a very dangerous and unhealthy belief that is held by most of us and is deeply rooted in societal expectations. And we must unlearn this before we can move forward and embrace the brave boundaries that are needed to stop living overwhelmed, exhausted, overcommitted, and unhealthy. If we do not recognize this belief as false and do not see that we are living our lives based on a false narrative, we cannot set down the guilt, anger, resentment, and insecurity that accompanies this belief and ask for help. We cannot set boundaries in our home that are much needed and accept the backlash that may accompany those boundaries, if we do not truly believe that domestic duties and child-rearing are shared responsibilities. And, I would argue, they are responsibilities that require MASSIVE help, humility, and a large dose of grace.

FACT: A society that says women can have careers (as long as they still do the dishes and take out the trash) is not a society that values women.

MULTITASKING MANIACS

Some of you may be struggling with this concept for two reasons; I know them because they are likely the same ones I struggle with. The first is that we women are excellent multitaskers. We women brag about this like we were born to multitask. I hear this all the time. *But Sasha, I can do ten things at once! At the end of the day, it is just easier if I do it all myself.* I am sure you can do a million things in a day, but it is not because you were born that way. It is because, as a girl, you were raised to see this modeled in your maternal figure, and so you have done the same. It is easier for you to do it, so why would you ask your partner or your kids to help out? Right?

The second reason that we as women take on the majority of domestic tasks, while also working ourselves to the bone in our careers, is because we do it well. Well yes, we do it well. If you have read Malcom Gladwell's book, *Outliers,* you know that anyone who does anything repetitively over and over learns to excel at it and perfect it.[xii] You become an expert in domestic duties. Congratulations! If domestic duties, child-rearing, and multitasking were the Olympics, every working woman I know would have a gold medal. You wake up and unconsciously, why you are waiting for the coffee to brew, change out the laundry, throw chicken in the crockpot, and pack a lunch before your partner has even turned on the shower. There is a reason you are good at this. You have been carrying this burden since you were ten. You are conditioned to do it all and make it look like you just walked into the kitchen to get coffee when, in fact, you have done twenty things. And then tonight, as you crash, you will ask yourself: *Why am I so tired, and what is wrong with me?*

Sound familiar? I hope I have convinced you that the problem with your work-life balance and your exhaustion does not simply lie in your professional career. My hope is that you now recognize how conditioned we are as women to take on our homes like they are our fortress, and we are the queen, responsible for all our constituents and running of the monarchy. Nothing is wrong with you; something may be wrong with your thoughts and the narrative you are living, but that, my friend, can be changed.

WHAT ARE BOUNDARIES?

In this book, we are going to get real and understand what boundaries are. We are going to jump forward with both feet into the deep waters of boundaries at work and at home. We are going to be open to changing our conscious minds, understanding that the boundaries that we need are different than what we may perceive them to be. For a boundary to work, we must understand that boundaries are not tools used to keep others out; rather, they are protective measures to keep our well-being centered.

Boundaries are:

- Kind
- Transparent
- Healthy
- Freeing
- Respectful
- Humble

Boundaries are kind because they tell others exactly what you can and cannot do in life, what you will and will not tolerate. They are kind because they are transparent. What I mean by this is that they don't leave people guessing on where they stand with you. Boundaries don't expect people we interact with to read our minds. They put the responsibility on us. If you do not tell someone your boundaries, well, then you do not have them. They are not there. You have not placed them in your life if no one can see them. Boundaries are healthy because they keep your ego in check. They remind you on the regular that you are human, and that, just like your cell phone, you won't work forever unless you are routinely recharged. Boundaries keep us free; they allow us to move in spaces where we are safe and well and keep us out of toxic spaces where our humanity is not respected. Boundaries clarify for us and those we do life with what we will and won't tolerate for our physical and mental well-being. And just like they teach others how to treat us, they teach us how to treat others. Boundaries are respectful. They humble us by their very nature to display to the world that we are precious cargo; our souls and hearts have limits. Our physical nature, while strong, needs sustenance, peace, and healing. Our mental health needs replenishing, recharging, and grace.

STEP ONE: BUILDING YOUR BOUNDARIES

Boundaries are life-giving. So why do we run from them? Because they take courage, especially as women, to create, explain, and cultivate. They require us to get uncomfortable and disappoint nice people. But do not worry, the people we care about the most will respect us for them and likely feel more comfortable teaching us their boundaries. Boundaries are a win-win. And if they aren't? Well, people who do not like or respect your boundaries are the very people for which you need to have them in the first place.

People who do not like or respect your boundaries are the very people for which boundaries need to exist.

So what boundaries do you need to develop first? Let's break them down into two main categories:

Professional Life Boundaries

- E-mail
- Work phone calls/texts
- Office hours/access interruptions
- Citizenship tasks (unpaid yet necessary tasks in the workplace)
- Vacation and time off
- Mentorship (coworkers and others)
- Socializing and networking events

Personal Boundaries

- Family interruptions
- Soul-care time
- Privacy/space

- Domestic duties

- Home upkeep

- Community commitments/volunteering

- Mentorship

- Social media/screen time

- Family members

- Friends

- Negative thoughts and behaviors

START WITH THE PAIN POINT

You may have read this list and thought, *Why do I need boundaries on all of these things?* It is unlikely you lack boundaries in every area of your life. But it is equally likely that you lack them in some major areas, as many of us do. In the next several chapters, we are going to evaluate why we need a boundary inventory and what boundaries we struggle with the most.

The best way to begin to evaluate the areas of your life where you need boundaries is to think of your largest pain point. Whether it is a person, a specific work area, or your inbox, whatever is causing you your largest amount of stress and exhaustion in life is probably where three things are true.

1. The pain point continues to fester because you lack boundaries around it.

2. You do not believe you have power over the issue to set boundaries.

3. You believe you should be able to handle it, without asking for help.

Did you let that sink in? Read it again. Most of the time, when we lack boundaries around our biggest pain point, we do not believe we have any power over whatever the pain point is. While we believe we are at the beck and call of, or under the control of whatever person or responsibility is our largest pain point, we simultaneously believe we have no power to say no or ask for help. Why do we believe this? Because we do not believe we are empowered to set healthy boundaries. We have given away our agency, while at the same time feeling guilty for attempting to take it back.

That may be hard for you to accept about yourself, but it is likely true. Have you ever complained about your weekend schedule or work schedule? The truth is that no one controls our time but us. We give others access to our calendar. We say yes to the job, and we remain working for the employers we choose. We tolerate how others treat us, or we don't tolerate it. It is a choice. We make the decision to answer work phone calls and e-mails after work. We choose to do all the laundry ourselves. It may seem like we have no other options, or there is no way out, but the truth is that we can determine how we spend our time, what we pour our energy into, and the boundaries we decide to live with or without.

You may be reading this and getting angry, thinking about a person or area you feel like you cannot control. It's true; there are many life circumstances out of our control, and we certainly have zero control over people's actions. But we can always choose how we allow people to treat us, our response to others' actions, and their behaviors toward us.

For example, I coach hundreds of women in my small-group coaching class, Brave Balance. One of the largest areas where women lack boundaries is in domestic duties. They do not see domestic duties as an area needing boundaries, yet they are constantly in conflict over home duties because the reality is that while they work full-time, 90 percent of the domestic duties fall to them. "I want to hire someone to help in our house, but my partner does not think we need it, and we disagree on this," is what I hear over and over from high-achieving women in my classes. Well, of course your partner does not think hiring someone is needed because the burden of responsibility does not fall on them. They don't feel the pain point. *Why? Because they have boundaries around what they will do, which you do not. They are not feeling the pain of doing 90 percent of the work, so why would they need to hire help? Their boundary has not been impacted, so they do not see the need.*

When I encourage women to set the boundary on what *they* can do in their home, suddenly there is work that needs to be done, which their partner suddenly realizes they themselves will have to do, which probably infringes on their boundary. And guess what happens next? You got it, there is an agreement on getting some help with the domestic or childcare duties causing the pain point.

As we move forward, mark this page. Look over the list of areas and decide where you lack boundaries, and what is your biggest pain point. You may not have recognized until now that your biggest boundaries may be needed in your home, or there *may be boundaries you lack within your own mind and behaviors.* Once you begin to consciously accept that boundaries are kind and acceptable, you can begin to embrace them. Think about your biggest pain point that causes you the most conflict and stress. Start there and ask yourself the questions below.

Boundary Checklist

1. Pick one area of your life that is your biggest pain point. It causes constant stress or strife. Maybe it is a work-related pain point, or maybe it is in your home.

2. When you think about this pain point, do you believe you have the power to control it? Why or why not?

3. What would creating a boundary around this pain point mean to you? Whom would you have to have honest conversations with to create the boundary?

4. What specific fears do you have about creating a boundary? Do you fear you will receive backlash or disappoint someone? Do you fear you won't be liked?

5. Imagine yourself setting the boundary and being free from the constant stress and/or exhaustion of this pain point. How would you feel to be free?

CHAPTER 3

CAN'T SOMEONE ELSE SAY NO FOR ME?

HOW BOUNDARIES HELP US TAKE BACK OUR POWER

Agency presupposes choice.[xiii]

—Jerome Bruner

The key to living your life with healthy boundaries is first to believe you are empowered to do so. We have to actually take the time and ask ourselves whether we truly believe we deserve boundaries, and then we must have the power to enforce our boundaries by educating others that they exist.

If you have read the challenging questions at the end of Chapter 2 but aren't quite sure if you truly believe you have the power to set boundaries, do not worry. In Chapter 3, we are going to go deep into the reasons why women are uncomfortable stepping into their power, claiming their agency, and believing they hold the power to set boundaries. Give yourself self-compassion; it is much more powerful than self-criticism in driving personal change. Most of us have never stopped to think about these questions such as, *Do I believe I have the power to say no and set firm boundaries?* Most of us have never stopped to think about this, because society expects women to say *yes.* Add that unspoken rule to life's responsibilities, and where is the time for self-reflection and growth? Our self-growth is marginalized to self-help books we hope to read on vacations or in the three minutes when we are sitting on the potty contemplating life's grand questions. But our questions don't materialize in our brain as thoughts such as, *Do I believe I have the power to say no?* Usually the questions we ask are: *What is wrong with me, and why am I so tired?* or *Why am I never in control of my day or my life?*

First, I want you to take a deep breath and give yourself grace. Remove any self-critical thoughts that are creeping in that are causing you to question your strength. You are strong, you are capable, and you are most likely what I call a "follow-througher." Why do I use this term? It's because people who show up and do what they say they are going to do are the people who desperately need boundaries. They are the people others know they can count on, and thus they are often overwhelmed with tasks and service to others. In a way, if you lack boundaries, it's because you are a person others rely on, which makes you a solid human being. A woman of her word. You aren't weak, you are dependable. You may lack boundaries, but you do not lack ethics. So, now we are going to figure out how to retrain your brain, step into your power, and realize *you can be both dependable and have strong boundaries.*

WHO IS SETTING YOUR BOUNDARIES

I want you to meditate for a moment on this truth:

If you do not set your own boundaries, someone else will be happy to set them for you.

You may be thinking, no way! Why would I give someone else power over may life, my daily calendar, my priorities? But guess what? You likely are. You do. You just have not recognized it. Let me explain.

One of the most monumental shifts in my thinking about my own boundaries (or lack thereof) came one cold, winter day at the top of a ski run in South Dakota. I was skiing with my family on our family spring break trip. My two little ones were in ski school, and my husband and I took the morning to ski with our two older boys. Our boys were pretty fearless skiers, having a shorter distance to fall and the ability to bounce up in less than two minutes after every wipe out. Not so for me. I was turning forty in a few months, and I remember each day on the slopes thinking, *I hope I don't injure myself today.* I desperately wanted to be part of the gang and ski with my crew. Each day my boys seemed to get more and more courageous and skilled and upped the ante taking on steeper runs. Every ski run became a little more treacherous and steeper, and my anxiety was going up by the hour. But instead of expressing my angst, I just pushed those thoughts away, thinking I was with my favorite people in the world, and I did not want to disappoint them.

I wanted to be the cool mom, the one who was fit enough to take on anything. I wanted them to see me as fearless, strong. After all, I was in pretty good shape. I could lift a lot of weight, as I had been doing CrossFit for several years. I was in good cardiovascular shape, and the skiing didn't wind me. Besides being physically able, I wanted to show them I was a fun mom.

The truth is that in the background there was a reason I convinced myself I should just go with the flow: I was often gone at work, missing things other moms with less demanding jobs could attend, and I constantly struggled with my own mountain of mom-guilt. How could I tell them that I actually didn't want to be with them on the slopes? Each day our runs were getting more stressful for me, and I was actually dreading the next one.

Also complicating things was that I was comparing myself to my husband, who was totally keeping up with them. Even if they beat him by a minute, he looked like a pro, swooshing to the bottom with a huge grin on his face. My husband, a natural athlete, is that person we all love to hate; he can literally figure out any sport if you give him an hour to practice. He is beyond coordinated and is uber competitive. On this vacation, he was winning major dad points on the slopes with the boys. They were laughing, ribbing each other, and having to wait for me at the end of each run. Meanwhile, as I meandered my way down the run, I begin to look like I had either a concussion or was intoxicated. I would ski for about twenty-five feet sideways, then switch back in an attempt to decrease the incline and slow my speed, stop at each side, then slowly turn, and do it again. As I skied (I am not sure that is even what you can call it) my stop-and-go approach all the way down, I would finally get to the bottom. I'd apologize, and they'd encourage me, saying, "You got this, Mom! Keep going! Let's do it again!" I would muster a fake smile, and through Lamaze-style deep breathing, find the words *Yes! Let's!* leaving my mouth.

Here is the thing about our lack of boundaries. There is always a reason, albeit a good one, why we refuse to set them. There's a reason why we dread to mention our own desires, wants, or needs, even if we are put in a situation that is unhealthy or unsafe. Here I was using my love for my kids and my value as a mother as the reason I was too afraid to say what was true, that skiing was not fun for me. It wasn't that I couldn't keep up physically, it was that I was constantly nervous I was going to injure myself. Instead, I just kept pushing.

Finally, we started on our last run of the day, the most difficult one yet. As my husband and I were riding the lift, I looked below at my legs dangling and the people squealing and swooshing down the run. I had this major realization that I did not want to do this next run. In fact, everything in me was saying *do not do this. Say no.* I looked at my husband, who was smiling and patting my leg, having a great time. I knew what I was about to say would come as a shock to him. I was nervous that I would ruin his day, our day, and the boys' memory. I was convinced my words would ruin our vacation.

BOUNDARIES RUIN EVERYTHING, DON'T THEY?

These were the thoughts that went through my mind. *I had convinced myself that expressing my boundary and saying no to this uber steep ski run would wreck our vacation.* I imagined in that moment my boys' sad faces, and my husband's disappointment. This was bad. Not to mention, how the heck would I get down the mountain? It is not like there was a stairway or an emergency exit labeled: "Scared mamas depart here!" I was going to completely derail the fun. The joy. All of it. What a buzz kill!

As we got off the lift and marched to the top to go down, before I could say a word, my boys were gone. One swoosh and they were giggling like mad, racing down the run. Suddenly, I found my voice. In that ride up the mountain, a few things became radically clear to me.

"Lance, stop," I said. My husband turned to me, preparing to push off.

"What's wrong?" he asked.

"I am not doing this run," I said, looking sad. He looked at me quizzically. I straightened my back and found my brave. "I am not doing it. I do not want to do this. It is not fun for me. I am scared I am going to hurt myself, and I am completely tachycardic and stressed."

He looked at me and said, "Okay."

I straightened my back and continued. "I am almost forty years old, and I've decided I am done doing things I do not want to do. I do not want to do anything I do not want to do, and I do NOT want to do this."

He stared at me for a few minutes in disbelief. I must have been hiding my fear well. "Okay Babe, but I am not sure how you are going to get down," he replied.

"I know, and I am not trying to be difficult, but this is not fun for me. It would be more fun for me to go back to the lodge and sip coffee while watching you all zip down."

In that moment, an angel appeared. A ski patrolman was skiing down and asked if I needed help. I called him my manna from heaven. I explained to him that I needed to get down the mountain, but not on my skis. He looked at me and smiled. "No problem. Take them off, and I will show you how to half walk/half slide down on your tush," he said. So that is what this nearly forty-year-old mama did. She took back her power and slid down a mountain on her tush. It was one of my better moments in life that, I am sure, will be shared around Christmas dinners for years to come.

Go ahead and laugh. I literally slithered down the steepest run, laughing my bum off. I told the ski patrolman about my "Aha" moment on the top of the lift, and that I was not longer doing things I didn't want to do just to please others. I told him I felt so free in claiming my boundaries, which apparently included not undergoing life-threatening ski runs that could put me in an ER with broken bones or a subdural hematoma. I was done.

My husband still talks about that moment. So do my boys. They said I looked SO embarrassing, but they also thought it was hilarious and still laugh about it. Guess what? It didn't ruin our vacation. It didn't scar their childhood vacation memories. It didn't make them think I was suddenly a weak, uncool, or unfit mother. After laughing with themselves and with me, they shrugged it off and moved on to asking what we were doing for dinner that night.

In that moment, there was a paramount shift in my thinking. *If I could not set boundaries and be honest with the people who loved me the most, how could I expect to set boundaries with my work colleagues, employees, or my community?* The truth is, I didn't think I had the power to set boundaries with my family. As they made plans, I would smile and go along with them. I let my two boys and my husband determine my plans for vacation, which included crossing major mental boundaries for me, because I didn't think I could say no without major ripples and disappointments.

I bring this up because I want you to see that for me—a cardiac anesthesiologist, a tenured professor, an acute-care physician who makes lifesaving decisions in major trauma and crisis—it was a BIG DEAL, a breakthrough moment to tell my tween boys and the love of my life that *I did not want to ski down a hill with them.*

Boundaries are not easy. Setting boundaries with those we love can make us feel like we are disappointing the most important people in our lives.

WHAT SCARES YOU ABOUT BOUNDARIES?

If you are judging yourself as you read this, or if you still aren't convinced you've got some tough internal work to do on your boundaries, I ask you to put yourself in my position on the mountaintop. If you know me in real life, you know I'm no pushover. I have no problem speaking up on behalf of others or myself. But I still had major boundary issues I had to work through. When I thought about it later that night, as I lay in bed in our cabin, I broke down some limiting beliefs that were keeping me from communicating and expressing my true wants and needs with those closest to me. Let's go through them so you can practice the same exercise with your pain points or with a boundary you need to set. Here's what my self-coaching that night went like.

1. Why was I afraid to set the boundary? *Because I was afraid of letting down my boys.*

2. Why would saying no to the hard ski runs let down my boys? *Because I am equating their love for me with me pleasing them and doing what they want.*

3. But I know they don't love me for what I do for them; they love me unconditionally as a mom. So, why was I feeling insecure as a mom? *Because I work long hours.*

4. Why am I angry at myself for setting this boundary? *Because I was comparing myself to Lance. Lance is more present with*

them. Lance gets to do more "fun" things with them. Lance is their favorite parent. They love him more.

5. Hmm . . . is that true? Do I actually think they love Lance more or that he is more fun? No. I am chasing an unobtainable goal—to always be present for our children and creating a story that they won't love me if I express my true feelings, which is that this dang hill is terrifying me. This is false.

TRUTH #1: I can't be there for every minute of their lives because I work to provide for them. They understand and love that I provide for them.

TRUTH #2: They do not love me for my skiing abilities, and they won't unlove me for my lack thereof.

TRUTH #3: Comparing myself to my husband is unhealthy for our marriage.

Okay. So, THIS is why I was afraid to set a boundary. This is what led me to do things that I didn't want to do, even if they were scary for me. I thought skiing with them would bring me more love, more favor, and be more pleasing to my children. I realized I was harboring some resentment toward my husband. I realized I was jealous of him. I realized I had some bitterness I had to let go of. I also realized I had every right to choose activities that would be fun for me to do with my children, and that their love didn't depend on me skiing down a mountain.

I told Lance the next morning at breakfast. We talked about how silly my connections had been and also that I wanted to do different things with them. I have a different role than their father, a very important one, and I offer them things he cannot. I had to stop comparing myself to someone who was not me. I had to start telling my family when I didn't want to do things. They would still love me.

A fantastic self-coaching exercise is to ask yourself why you may be afraid to speak openly to work colleagues or family members about your boundaries. Here are a few questions to get you thinking about why you may be resistant to setting boundaries and telling people your true wants and desires. When we understand our why, we can understand our internal resistance to being transparent with others about our own needs, and we can then work to remove that resistance.

1. Why do you fear telling others *no?* Do you feel you will only be liked for your ability to serve others?

2. At some point in our lives, we are often conditioned or taught as young girls that we must be obedient, which means saying *yes* to please others. Think of a time where perhaps you were disciplined for saying no or disappointing another person by voicing your own want or need. Often, we may instantly feel shame when we go back to that memory, and shame is an extremely powerful emotion that we try to avoid at all costs. Are your avoiding setting a boundary in order to avoid a feeling of shame? Why?

3. Think of your best friend. If your best friend told you *no* to something you asked him or her to do, would you shame them? Most likely you would not. So ask yourself, do you have a false belief that others may shame you for setting a boundary, or that you would be a "bad" person for voicing your own needs? We can't control another's response, but most likely, if someone is shaming us for taking care of ourselves and setting boundaries around our well-being, they do not have our best

interests in mind. The next question should be, *why do I care what this person thinks of me? Do I think my internal validation and worth are based on another person's idea of what I should be or what I should do?*

HOW TO THINK CRITICALLY ABOUT YOUR BOUNDARIES

Now I want you to think about yourself. Maybe you are thinking you would have no problem telling your love-people you weren't going to ski with them. Maybe you are having a hard time relating to yourself in my story. I want to challenge you to ask yourself these simple yet powerful questions. They will reveal your thoughts regarding boundaries and get to the why behind your lack of boundaries.

- How often do you find yourself doing something you don't want to do?

- How often do you find yourself without time for yourself at the end of each day?

- How often do you say *yes* to something you don't want to spend time or resources on in order to please others?

- How comfortable are you saying *no* to others without guilt?

- How often do you find yourself making excuses or lying about why you *can't* participate in something, when in reality you *don't* want to do it?

- How often do you find yourself over committing to people at home or in your workplace to "make up" for saying *no*?

- How often to you find yourself taking on work projects you are not interested in or paid to do, simply to please others?

- How often do you find yourself volunteering for things you aren't passionate about simply to avoid confrontation?

These questions are really meant to make you stop and take inventory of your own need to please and your own thoughts about having the ability, and therefore the power, to say *no*. When you hear the words "peer pressure," do you instantly think of junior high? If you are like me, you probably think of the time some awkward eighth grader asked you to share your answers on the math test or sneak out some alcohol stored in his parents' basement. We don't tend to think about experiencing peer pressure as adults. We think that succumbing to peer pressure is something we may have last experienced in college or that long-ago bachelorette party trip. We chalk up peer pressure we experience in adulthood to "people-pleasing." But isn't it the same thing?

It may be easy to turn down shotgunning a beer when we are in our forties. But it isn't as easy to say no to volunteering for school events, taking on unpaid work that has to be done in our workspaces, or telling our family we are going to start going to the gym in the morning and need to go to bed an hour earlier in order to put our health first. But if you think about it, having zero boundaries as an adult is really no different than caving to pressure in junior high.

You may be thinking, "Well, Sasha, this kind of peer pressure isn't as dangerous." Clearly you have never heard of "death by committee."

One of the best ways to save yourself from caving to peer pressure in junior high was to have a buddy with you who would resist with you. You'd stare at each other and give each other the "eyes," you know, the one that would say, "You say *no!*" while the other said, "No, YOU!" You knew the best way to get out of whatever bad idea someone was proposing was to stick together. You'd look at your loudest friend, hoping she'd speak up and say no for all of you. When she did pipe up, and say, "Nah, we are moving on to the next thing," you'd breathe a sigh of relief. Whew. You escaped narrowly, and you didn't have to do the thing you knew you didn't really want to do and wasn't healthy for you.

WHERE IS MY FAIRY GODMOTHER?

Wouldn't it be nice if someone could do that for us now, as adults? If someone could sweep in and say nope, she doesn't have time for that, because it is not good for her. Or, sorry, she's busy and doesn't work for free. We tend to wish for a savior to make it easier, where we do not have to initiate boundary-setting conversations with those who may reject them. Many times we must set boundaries for people who have come to depend on us for encouragement or emotional support. Maybe we have become that person's mentor or the person they can vent to. We don't know how to set the boundary, so we avoid it and wish for a fairy godmother who will set it for us.

But if you've read my book *Between Grit and Grace,* you know we do not need a fairy godmother; we have the strength within ourselves as women to have uncomfortable conversations and do what is right for our own health. In my Brave Balance class, I teach high-achieving professional women how to step into their power by reorganizing their priorities. Through the twelve-week class, we start with an assessment of identifying areas that are burning us out as working women and move through the course with solid tactics to set fierce boundaries. By the end of the course, the outcomes are incredible. Women have stopped taking on unpaid work. They have set clear boundaries with e-mail and text messaging during non-work hours. Some have asked for raises and received promotions. Some have found the courage and clarity to leave toxic work environments and relationships. They have hired people to help them in their homes to allow them time for themselves. All have made daily time with themselves a habit.

One of the women in my coaching class was really struggling to set a boundary with a coworker, and I remember her saying she felt embarrassed and guilty as she explained the situation. While some women were sharing stories of sexual discrimination and bias in the workplace, she felt her struggle was less important. As I led the group coaching session through her sharing, all of the women had some major "Aha" moments come to life.

Her struggle was with a junior coworker who came into her office, at the same time every day, to vent about work frustrations and ask her for advice. My client was a mentor to this woman. She really liked her junior colleague and wanted to help her succeed. The problem was that this woman would wait for my client to have her first break in her day between patients, plop down in my client's office, and take thirty minutes of precious time my client would use to catch up on patient charting and tasks. Sometimes, the junior woman would stay for forty-five minutes, which resulted in my client staying late at the end of every work night to catch up after patients. My client would often miss the narrow window to share dinner with her kids before their activities or see her family before the "second shift" of home responsibilities began. It was exhausting and frustrating her, but she didn't know how to change what had become a daily habit without hurting her colleague's feelings or inciting anger and disappointment.

"She may be disappointed when you express your boundary," I explained. "She may become angry. She may be hurt," I coached. My client didn't like those answers. She wanted me to tell her how to set the boundary without all of the repercussions. The truth is, we can't control other people's reactions, and we can't expect people to not be upset or disappointed when remove a part of ourselves we've been giving them free of charge, whenever they needed it, for a long time. When we allow people to take what they need from us, without giving them any indication it is costing us something, how can we expect them to be happy when we stop doing it? Oftentimes, the person has no idea that our lack of boundaries is costly to us or is something we actually need to set clear expectations or fences around.

TRUTH: You cannot expect people who've been receiving the gift of you having zero boundaries with them to react happily when that gift goes away.

A boundary that only lives in your head is not a boundary.

Let's repeat that. If you only "wish" someone to pay you for your work, respect your nonwork hours, or respect your work hours to limit work interruptions, that is not setting a boundary. A wish is not a boundary. It is simply that: an imaginary want, desire, or hope for an outcome. You are wishing for someone to read your mind. You have not set the boundary, you have only wished for it. How can we expect people to know our boundaries? We can't.

TRUTH: Your boundary is not a boundary until it is communicated to the people who will be affected by it.

Boundary setting isn't easy. There's no simple fix or consultant you can call in to fix the boundary for you. You can't ask someone else to communicate the boundary for you. You also cannot expect people who are hearing about your boundary setting for the first time to celebrate the change. However, you do have the power and the agency to set your boundaries, and you can and will survive the backlash, the uncomfortableness, and the fallout of the change.

My client finally set a time to confront her coworker and explain how she needed to set clear boundaries of when she could mentor her and listen to her. When having a difficult conversation about boundary setting, I always encourage people to confront head on their fears. My client's fear was that she would hurt her coworker, whom she deeply cared about as evidenced by her availability to her 24/7. So, I had her list all the ways she valued her coworker and to start the conversation with the truth: boundaries were needed to improve their relationship and because she valued her friend. She told her she valued her, she enjoyed mentoring her, and she wanted to continue their relationship. My client then assumed positive intent, which is the best way to go into a difficult conversation. Often, we make conversations so much worse in our mind than they actually are. By telling her coworker that she was confident she would understand, she removed the fear from the conversation. My client explained that their daily talk was causing her to stay late at the end of each day to finish the work she had to do. My client told her she wants to continue to mentor her but needed to set up a new process to do so. She suggested having a weekly, rotating appointment, and if she had concerns, they could meet for fifteen minutes, and she would be best prepared for how to address them. Guess what? It worked. Her coworker was disappointed, but with space and time, it worked itself out. And more importantly, my client was modeling boundaries for her coworker. When we set boundaries with others, we teach them it is okay to set boundaries with us and with others.

YOUR MOST PRECIOUS ASSET

I put this example in this book because it is real life. It is just as important as putting boundaries around unpaid work. Time is the most important gift we are given in this life. It is costly, and it is precious. If you think of your biggest pain point, as I challenged you to do in Chapter 2, I guarantee it involves time. Think of your time as a precious commodity. Now, what is the most special, materialistic thing you own? Is it your home? Your car? A special piece of jewelry? An heirloom? Would you give these things away with no instructions? Would you let someone use them whenever and however they wanted? Probably not. Your time is SO much more important than that. Your health and your most important relationships depend on your ability to manage and protect your time.

You can set boundaries when it comes to your time. Let your mind start to think about those conversations about boundaries. How does it make you feel? Where would you need to begin? Just think about it. And like my Brave Balance class, keep going. Keep reading. We will get there.

Boundary Check-In

1. What is an area of your work life in which you lack boundaries and find yourself wishing for a boundary around this subject?

2. What person(s) is most affected by the lack of your boundary?

3. What is the exact boundary you would need to set to move from stress to peace?

4. What would a conversation with the person(s) look like?

5. What fears do you have when you think of having a boundary-setting conversation?

CHAPTER 4

WHATEVER YOU DO, DO NOT LOOK THEM IN THE EYE

WHY SETTING A BOUNDARY FEELS UNCOMFORTABLE

You wouldn't worry so much about what others think of you if you realized how seldom they do.

—Unknown

When you ask others how easy it is for them to set boundaries, the majority of people will simply stare back at you. Most people do not know what boundaries are. Boundaries sound like some form of midlife psychobabble daytime TV hosts break down for lazy people who find themselves in unhealthy relationships. Boundaries are not for us; we are high-functioning women. Why do we need boundaries? Those people who are aware of what boundaries are typically do not describe them as favorable or something they look forward to setting with others. When I think about setting a boundary, I think of a hundred other things I would rather do, including mountain loads of teenage boys' laundry. Most of us do not recognize that our baseline exhaustion, blurred lines between work and home life, and guilt we carry for not being "enough" likely results from our lack of boundaries. Whether it is personal relationships with others, or even the work we do to earn our salaries, boundaries are critical for success.

BOUNDARIES: A LEARNED BEHAVIOR

It is important to note that boundaries are not something we learn as we grow older. Like most behaviors, they are modeled for us. So, if we lack boundaries, or we have never thought of them, or we are terrified to set them, we likely have these thoughts because we have learned them or have seen them modeled by others in our lives.

As women, we model much of our behavior based on our maternal figure: our mother, our grandmother, or the woman who influenced us the most in life. Most of how we've learned to act, negotiate, or how NOT to act we learned by watching our maternal figure. If our mother was not afraid to set strong boundaries and demonstrated this, we likely are more comfortable setting boundaries without guilt. If we watched our mother serve everyone, do everything in our home, and rarely say *no* or ask for help, we may find ourselves in the middle of our lives doing the same. At the same time, if we are a person who has problems respecting other people's boundaries, this likely means no one set boundaries for us as children. Maybe we grew up in a home where boundaries were not enforced or were seen as restrictive, so we have a problem following the boundaries other people set for us.

TRUTH: Most of us develop our belief system about boundaries from our maternal figure.

It is important to think about our belief system about boundaries. Before we can identify why boundaries make us uncomfortable, we have to dig deep and think about the reasons we avoid boundaries. We have to investigate where the idea that boundaries are bad or that we just aren't the type to set boundaries came from. As my friend Karin says, we have to "launch an investigation." Buckle up, Buttercup. This is going to be fun!

When I think about my own life, there are some things that have followed me from my childhood into adulthood. No matter how hard I tried to leave some things behind, or how many times I would think to myself, "when I am a mom, I am NEVER doing that to my kids!" certain behaviors, beliefs, and words found their way out of my mind and replicated themselves in how I parented my kids. So, it is not surprising to think that other behaviors, such as teaching people how to treat us, also find their way into our adulthood behaviors.

When I was growing up, my younger sister Leah and I shared a room. For years we had a double bed, and we slept together every night. When my oldest sister moved out, I was SO excited to get my own room. Finally, I could sleep by myself! No more Leah waking me up every night telling me she was scared. No more Leah asking me to scratch her back each night. No more Leah asking me to hold her hand because she heard a noise. *Goodbye, Leah Marie.* I was ten when I moved into my new room and decorated it pale blue. I had a dial phone the color of ice blue I was so proud of. I had an ice-blue colored alarm clock where I would listen to the "Top 9 and 9" until

Mom would open the door and tell me to go to bed. No more dolls, no more Barbies! I was moving up!

The first night, I couldn't wait to go to sleep. As I was getting ready for bed, I found Leah standing in the doorway. "I am scared," she said. "Leah, you have your own room. You can't sleep with me," I firmly stated. She started begging me. I held firm. It lasted maybe ten minutes until she wore me down. "Okay, just for tonight," I said.

Except that is not how it went. Every night she would ask me, and every night I'd cave. Occasionally, I'd find some inner strength and tell her no. She'd go door to door and beg my older sister, our parents, and end up crying outside my door. I'd let her in. I don't think Leah slept in her own bed until she was twelve years old. She never had to make her bed. It stayed perfectly made and unslept in for several years until she grew up and decided she was more comfortable in her own room. As I type this, I am laughing out loud. I can see her in her footie pajamas. I also see now that she is absolutely correct. Leah Marie says whenever I want to tell a funny story at a party, I tell a story about her from our childhood. And now Leah's childhood story has made it into my book.

Before I had kids, I told my husband, Lance, that we were never allowing our kids to sleep with us. Under no circumstances would they sleep in our room. Once they were out of the bassinette, they were sleeping in their crib. When each of my newborns turned twelve weeks old, I started putting them in their own room at night to sleep. When we moved into our second home, their rooms were on a different level. "You aren't going to put that newborn all the way upstairs away from you, are you?" my mom asked one day.

"Yes, Mom, I am," I answered. "But they are so far away! You are going to have to walk so far for each nightly feeding," my mom said.

"I know. I can do it," I answered. Even my husband was skeptical, and it was quite a jaunt to reach them at one in the morning.

But I held the line. No matter how many times my babies got up in the night, I would get up, climb the stairs, walk down the hallway, and comfort them or feed them in their rooms. I never caved. And it stayed that way for their entire childhood. It did not matter if they came in sick, ill, scared, or upset. I would take them back to their rooms, sit in their room, or lay on the floor, but I never let them sleep with me. If they were sick, I'd stay in their room on the floor or sit on their bed and rub them back to sleep. I'd sit in the hallway and listen to them breathe, but I never once let any of my kids sleep with me. I remember one night that Lance and I were both exhausted after being up all night with our fourth child, Levi, who had a bad case of croup. [If you have four kids, bless you. There is something that happens when you cross the four line. It is like a weariness that seeps deep into your bones, and you just surrender to the fact you will in fact be terminally tired.] Lance gave me the look. I knew this look as I had seen it many times. With his face, he was saying, *Can't he just sleep with us?* No, I answered back, with my eyes. "I will sit upstairs in his room," I said.

The next morning, as we were both dragging ourselves to get ready for work at 5:30 AM after little sleep, Lance said "WHY are you like this? Why is this such a harsh line with you? The no-sleeping-in-our-bed rule?" I couldn't answer him. I didn't know.

It took me a few days of pondering to figure it out. Leah. My precious little sister. For a long time, before my sister Amy came along, Leah was the baby. It was easy to have very few boundaries with her. We let Leah Marie get away with many things, as babies often do, mostly, because my parents were tired. When it was 10:00 PM and everyone was completely exhausted, Leah would ask if she could sleep with me, and we'd cave. My parents didn't have the energy to make her sleep in her own room, and I didn't have the heart to say *no*. When my own kids came along, I was adamant they were NOT going to sleep with anyone but themselves in their own beds. Everyone would be in their own space. I was strict; stricter than I probably had to be. Even when they were sick, and I could have made them a bed on the floor and saved myself several hours of sleep and treks up the stairs, I couldn't do it. My childhood influenced my adulthood. I had this limiting belief that if I let them sleep with me once, it would be forever. I was afraid of having to set the boundary over and over, so I didn't allow for any give. No bend.

LOOKING BACK TO MOVE AHEAD

Sometimes we have to go back to go forward. We may have fears, false or wrong beliefs that feed our lack of boundaries. Often, we have made-up "rules" for ourselves that we have created and cling to when there may be no apparent reason. Let's dig into some common false beliefs that may be limiting your ability to move forward and create life-giving boundaries you desperately need. At one time or another, I've held most of these false beliefs myself and wrestled with them as I tried to rewire the pathways of my brain and replace them with what I knew to be true. False beliefs can be deep in our minds, and we tend to go to them fast, because they are easy. They are often the path of least resistance, and we may find ourselves embracing them as easily as our favorite slippers and flannel pajamas in winter. There's a reason we keep them around; they feel good.

In the next section, we are going to unpack six common false beliefs that often prevent us from believing that we can and should welcome fierce boundaries in our daily lives. Through coaching hundreds of women in my classes, these six reasons are quoted over and over by highly successful women who find themselves burned out and beaten up by life by trying to do it all. As you read through each of them, I challenge you to dig deep and sit with each false belief for a while. Ask yourself the hard questions: Do you identify with any of these beliefs? Where did you learn a particular belief? How has this belief served you thus far?

SIX COMMON FALSE BELIEFS ON BOUNDARIES

For most of us, when we think about boundaries, we automatically do a deep sigh. In our minds, boundaries are hard. They are uncomfortable. They are difficult, for us and for others who are affected by our boundaries. We have to stop for a minute and take a deep breath. We have to bring boundaries to the front of our minds, which can be exhausting if we believe they are rough at the baseline. Most of us do not go through our days seeing our conflict, our stress, or our work through the lens of boundaries. The number one false belief we have is that boundaries have nothing to do with our daily overwhelm or exhaustion. So, the number one false belief we have about boundaries in our daily life is actually that:

1. We don't recognize a boundary has been crossed.

We do not see that daily work interruptions, interpersonal conflicts, parenting stress, or our never-ending to-do list is likely causing us major stress and angst in life because we lack boundaries or a boundary in our mind has been crossed that we've never expressed to those we do life with. Stay with me.

I have a friend who, for years, let her children interrupt her on the phone. She could never talk on the phone even if it was five-minute conversation. It was like the minute she got on the phone, I would hear: "Mommy, Mommy, Mommy!" nonstop. I would start my sentence for the third time and get interrupted by her children. Finally, I stopped calling her. I would text her. And when she would reach out in need of some coaching, I finally had to say, "I find it really hard to talk to you when your kids are home."

She responded, "My kids just won't let me talk on the phone. I've told them so many times, and they do not listen. My kids just aren't the kind that let me talk."

I didn't want to tell her what I knew was true: her kids didn't allow her to talk on the phone, because she had ZERO boundaries for them to follow. None. She would talk over them and say, "I am on the phone!" which did nothing. My friend was convinced her kids were just worse than the norm and couldn't learn boundaries at a young age. She was convinced everyone else's kids were just "born better." Um, no.

Kids can learn boundaries. Believe me. I have four. If you think about it, it is somewhat insulting to our children to act like they can't learn boundaries. My kids, at age two, could work my iPhone better than I could. I am 99 percent certain that if I needed them to connect me with the embassy in Ukraine, my kids could figure it out. They are brilliant with technology. You are telling me they can't learn to be quiet, or move to another room, or stay out of the room you are in when you are on the phone?

I remember gently mentioning to my friend that she needed to give them clear boundaries for phone time. "Boundaries?" she asked. She acted like I suggested she hand them matches and gasoline.

Most of the time when we are frustrated, whether due to work or home, it is because someone has an expectation we are not meeting or someone is not meeting our expectation. And 99 percent of the time, it is because we do not realize we need boundaries. We either must communicate that boundary to someone or, even more importantly, we must communicate it to ourselves. If we do not recognize that a boundary has been crossed, or that we have not communicated a boundary to others or ourselves, we cannot begin the work of identifying and setting boundaries. If you have a big pain point at work, I guarantee you that you lack boundaries regarding it. So stop for a minute and think: have you identified one to three boundaries that pain point needs to move the needle toward control and peace? Take a moment and write them down.

It is important to note that identifying where to begin may take time. One of my clients, Dr. A, is a family medicine physician in a large private practice and busy mom of two. When she first attended one of my retreats, she sat in front of me the first day, quietly smiling up at me while I spoke on boundaries. As the morning went on, and we got into more specifics on how to identify symptoms of burnout, I noticed silent tears streaming down her cheeks. She was completely and totally burned out and emotionally empty. She was suffering more than she realized, and while she desperately needed boundaries to reclaim her well-being, she didn't know where to start.

"I remember you saying to us 'Your biggest pain point is the place you lack the most boundaries,'" Dr. A says. "While I knew

I desperately needed to start somewhere, it was another year before I figured out what my biggest pain point was. I was so overwhelmed and burned out in life, I could not figure out where the actual problem was and where to begin," she explained.

"Once I started to realize I needed to set radical boundaries around my charting and my e-mail, it was so freeing. Because I had strong boundaries, I knew I needed to hire a virtual scribe, change expectations of response time for those in my office, and let others know I would no longer be taking work home with me each evening," Dr. A explained. "Boundaries allowed me to stop spending my entire night working. The work I have done with Brave Enough showed me I have the power to change circumstances in my life, but only if I am willing to spend time with myself to figure out what boundaries I need. For years I went through life with my head down, just getting through my day, not taking the time feel or think about what was wrong. Now I know I need time alone to sit and process for me to be the healthiest version of me," she said.

Like Dr. A, it may take you a year to identify what biggest boundaries you lack and how to enforce them. Be kind to yourself. Setting boundaries is not a race, and you aren't behind. Just the fact you are here, taking the time to read this work, means you are already ahead.

2. We believe setting boundaries is "just not our personality."

Have you ever wished you were a stronger, more direct, braver person, the kind for whom boundary setting is easy? Have you ever thought to yourself: I wish I could set a boundary, or tell this person what I will and won't tolerate, but I am just not that type of person? Okay. Deep breath and a whopping dose of grace. Because I am about to get real here and give you a little love smack. What you mean is that YOU CHOOSE not to be that type of person. If you believe boundaries are hard, or that boundaries are mean, then who would want to set boundaries? No one! But if you believe boundaries are kind because they protect our well-being and the well-being of others, then you are basically saying to yourself, *"I am not the kind of person who can be kind."*

It is really no different than saying to yourself, "I am not an athlete, so I cannot exercise." We've all made these types of excuses for ourselves. Maybe you are not the most coordinated or athletic person in the room, but that does not mean you can't take a thirty minute walk every day and work up a sweat. Yes, some people have personalities where it is easier for them to say no, set boundaries, and deal with the backlash. But that does not mean you, as a unique person with traits and motivations and fears of your own, cannot learn to set boundaries. When you believe the limiting belief that, "I am unable to set boundaries because it is just not in my personality," you are limiting yourself, choosing a life of overwhelm and burnout, and limiting your power.

3. We believe it is easier to live boundary free.

This is a foundational limiting belief that we hold on to. We take the path of least resistance, because we are convinced it is easier. It is easier to just do the thing others have asked of us than to set the boundary. It is easier to respond to the work text at 10:00 PM than not respond and explain why you didn't tomorrow in the office. It is easier to do the unpaid work, than to tell your supervisor you will be happy to do the work if you are paid for it. It is easier to do the laundry and clean the house for hours each Saturday, than to assign tasks to those you live with and face the backlash. It is easier to skip your workout each morning than hire someone to come in the mornings to help with breakfast and school run and face backlash or uncomfortable conversations from those who may judge you. It is easier to let the coworker interrupt you daily than to explain what your door being shut means.

The most common limiting belief we have is that it is less hassle to just accept that someone isn't respecting our boundaries than it is to enforce them. We take the path of least resistance. We remain compliant. We remain a doormat. We remain silent. We avoid critical conversations. We avoid honest discussions with those who cross our boundaries. It is just easier this way. We are more likeable when we do what others expect of us and don't enforce our boundaries.

That is true, we are much more liked when we have no boundaries. I have said it once, and I will say it a thousand times: the world runs on women with no boundaries. It is how the world continues to turn. Think of the gender pay gap: Can you imagine what would happen if women stopped doing work for free? Who would do the work? How would corporations, health systems, teaching institutions, etc., go on? They wouldn't. They expect women to work for free. (Because guess what: Working for "less" is actually working for FREE. Part of the job women do is uncompensated, or how else do you explain the hundreds of studies that show men get paid more to do the same job?)

TRUTH: The world runs on the backs of women with no boundaries.

We have to intentionally remove the belief that it is easier to live without boundaries than to live with them. To do so means we remove the belief that it is better to be overworked, underpaid, burned out, and LIKED, than it is to have work-life control, do work we are fairly paid to do, live well, face backlash for stepping in our power, and be respected. Think of your pain point, and ask yourself: what part of this issue is fueled by a desire to be liked and a fear of being unliked, than it is to be respected?

I am not saying that setting boundaries is easy; it is not. It requires energy and intention. But until you believe in learning how to identify the boundaries that need to be set, and that setting them is worth the effort, the overwhelm in your life won't change.

I know many women whom I have encouraged to set much needed boundaries, who are being taken advantage of, or who have other people robbing them of their time or priorities, who can't bring themselves to set boundaries. They can't find the energy or the courage, as they believe building fences will be too painful, difficult, or stressful. So, they continue on until they burn out.

The truth is that boundaries often lead us down a path of great success and innovation. Here's an example: For the first few years of building my online community, I received several requests in my direct messaging for advice. At first, when my group was five hundred, I could answer them daily. I gave advice on everything from how to negotiate for a raise, to how to leave an abusive marriage, to how to report and navigate bias and discrimination. I somehow found myself in this position where I felt a responsibility to women I had never met but wanted to help. When the group grew, to thousand, then three-thousand, and eventually to thirteen-thousand women physicians, I couldn't keep up with my direct messages. Most of the time I would save them for Friday nights or Saturday mornings, when I would wake up early to read and respond. I would open the messages and find some were time sensitive—women had an important meeting they wanted advice on, and I had missed it. Or they were in a terrible situation at work or home and needed advice, and I hadn't been there for them. Many of them would express disappointment in me for my lack of response and attention. This led to anxiety if I didn't check and respond more than once a week. I started to evaluate the time I was spending, and it was anywhere between thirty minutes and one hour each day answering women and giving advice—at the expense of my family, my health, and my sleep.

I hired a business consultant to help me manage some other aspects of my business, and she started probing into my time management. "You personally answer direct messages asking for advice?" Yes, I responded. I told her I liked helping women, but I couldn't figure out how to manage it. "You need boundaries," she said. I had no idea what she was talking about.

"But I am HELPING these women," I argued. She explained to me that helping others at the expense of my own health and well-being was in fact, unhealthy and not very bright.

"I just wish they would only expect me to answer them maybe once a week, and not when I am on vacation," I said.

She laughed. "Sasha, they are not mind readers. You have no boundaries, so of course everyone knows they can directly message you whenever about whatever, and you will respond," she explained.

She was right. I just couldn't imagine letting women down. But

I knew I had to undo the mess I had created. I still wanted to help women, but my consultant challenged me to write down some basic structure of what helping women should look like, and how it would remain healthy. She asked me one question that really shook me. "Would you ever message a woman leader and ask her for advice and be upset that she didn't message you back?" The truth is, I wouldn't. I would not be upset, I would be grateful if anyone helped me in any way. There were several women in my field who I would reach out to on occasion and post a question over e-mail, and I never expected an answer but was always thankful for any advice they offered. More importantly, I believed in paying women for their time and expertise, and I myself had paid several women experts for the coaching and consultation. Why did I think that I myself didn't have value or expertise similar to the women I hired? That was a deeper question and took me some time to dive into. Many of my limiting beliefs stemmed from things I had heard others say about me, or criticism I had received for even starting a community of women.

This exercise in boundary setting grew something powerful: it allowed me to create a class for women who were experiencing similar obstacles. Boundaries can lead to innovation by forcing us to think of ways around obstacles differently. I found a way for women to consult my expertise for thirty minutes or an hour in a scheduled, controlled timeframe. I stopped responding to every message that took me away from being a present parent. I stopped looking at my phone 24/7. I felt *free*. I was able to coach a smaller group of women on a deeper level and help them at a serious level, backed with data and science, as I created the curriculum for the class. And the best part? The women wanted to be there and wanted my help, which I did during specific hours. I lost some followers, and some women in my group were angry with my boundary, but guess what? I not only survived, I thrived. I learned that not everyone would understand my reasoning. In fact, people with zero boundaries do not understand people with boundaries.

It is not for them to understand. They are your boundaries, not theirs. We cannot expect others to understand our lives, our priorities, or our time management.

TRUTH: We cannot expect people with zero boundaries to understand people with boundaries.

4. We believe we have to say yes to everything.

Often, the foundation of our resistance to implementing boundaries is that we go into conversations, respond to e-mails, and open text messages with the expectation that we will say yes to whatever it is we are being asked to do. We women have the baseline assumption that our go-to response is yes. To say *no* is a deviation from normalcy. We are expected to say *yes,* and we expect other women to say yes. If you don't believe me, think about the last time someone approached you with a task that you could do, but didn't want to do, because it did not align with your current priorities or bring you joy. Instantaneously, you put it in the joy versus dread meter, and it brought dread, not joy. Before the person finished their sentence where they were asking you for something, you already knew you didn't want to do it. However, you didn't feel comfortable or ready to say no, so you responded like this:

- That sounds great! I will think about it.

- Thanks for asking me, I will let you know!

- Awesome. I will get back to you.

- I'll check my calendar and e-mail you soon.

- Sure, I can do that, just let me check on a few things first.

Sound familiar? Have you ever said these things out loud or written them in an e-mail, while at the same time KNOWING your true answer, if you could be honest, is a resounding *NO!?*

Our baseline answer when asked to do things we do not want to do is "maybe." And then we procrastinate saying *no* by waiting to respond, causing our final answer to more likely to be a yes to the thing we want to say *NO* to. Here is something I tell my students in my classes: saying no today is less painful than saying *no* tomorrow. It's true.

So why don't we say *no?* We don't say *no* because the baseline foundation is that women say *yes.* Remember limiting belief 3 above: We actually think it is easier to say yes to something we have zero desire to do, or to allow people to cross our boundaries, than to say *no* immediately and set boundaries instantaneously.

Here is the byproduct of saying *yes* when we want to say *no:* anger. We experience repressed anger at the person or group for ASKING us to participate. How dare they! Don't they know how busy we are? Don't they see and respect our boundaries? Why did they even ask us? They KNOW we will say yes, even when we do not want to do it. We become angry. We get internally mad, and we repress it until we become increasingly frustrated and blow up. Then we may come home, snap at our kids, yell at our partner, and blame it on a stressful day.

Why? Because we are angry at others for not respecting our invisible boundaries and leaving us alone. We are angry at others

for not reading our minds. We are angry at others sometimes before
they even ask.

**Tough love moment: Your anger is on YOU. If someone simply
asking you to take on something makes you angry, you don't have
boundaries, and you do not feel empowered to protect them.**

Have you ever actually avoided people because you fear them
asking you for something or crossing a boundary? I know, I know.
We must stop avoiding people because we are afraid they will ask
us to do something. That is being a boundary avoider. Boundary
avoiders operate under the limiting belief that they must say *yes* to
others' expectations, that they must welcome all who enter into their
professional and personal life with any agenda at any time, because
this is what women are expected to do.

I remember a time early in my career when I was asked to give a
lecture on a specific pediatric disease in anesthesia. As a young, rel-
atively unknown academic, I was flattered by the invitation to speak
nationally. But I had zero interest in the topic. I didn't want to leave
my young kids and spend my precious meeting days at a conference
where I'd likely not gain much as a cardiac anesthesiologist. I asked
a more senior colleague if saying no would be appropriate, given my
lack of interest in the topic.

"You may not get asked again," he replied.

I felt trapped. He was right, I may not get asked again. I felt like
I needed to speak on the topic to ensure I was seen as hardworking
and serious. The problem with this entire scenario is that every time
I said *yes* early in my career to opportunities that didn't fit my actual
career interests and plan, two things began to spiral. One, I found
success in these arenas, and I would then be asked to do the NEXT

thing, making it even harder to say *no*. When you are a person who shows up and completes a job well, guess what? You get asked again. And again. Early in my career I found myself often succeeding in areas for which I had little interest, simply because someone asked me to do something, and I showed up, did it, and did it well.

The second problem this caused for me was that saying yes to every opportunity or task that didn't light my soul on fire utilized brain space, energy, and precious time I could have focused on work that actually interested and excited me.

It took me about five years before I realized I had few professional boundaries, which meant I had little professional focus. I was extremely motivated, hardworking, and wanting to climb the academic ladder. I mistakenly thought saying yes to every opportunity or request would put me on the fast track to success. What it put me on was the fast lane to burnout. If you've read my book *Between Grit and Grace*, you know what happened next. It wasn't pretty.

We have to remove the limiting belief that saying no to another's expectations of us or to every opportunity or request from others is abnormal, rude, lazy, inconsiderate, wrong. We must stop thinking boundaries make us seem indifferent, unlikable, unfriendly, or selfish. We must stop getting angry at others for asking us to do things and instead see it as a compliment. But we must unbind the two: just because someone asks you do something does not mean you must say yes to be grateful. You are likely being asked to do something because you are a woman who gets things done. You show up, you do good work. Accept the compliment and give the answer you want. Does it bring you joy or dread? If we want to live our lives for our priorities, we must be women who have no problem setting boundaries and no guilt in saying no. Don't worry, by the end of this book you will be that woman.

5. We are bone tired. We are too tired to set the boundary.

If you are exhausted, setting a boundary seems a monumental task. It feels like someone has asked you to run a marathon when you don't have a 5K in you. I believe that the number one reason we don't set boundaries is simply this: we are completely, utterly worn out. We come to the end of our day or week and are so tired that we can't find the energy to say *no, I can't do that.* When our boss hands us work that someone else gets paid to do, we do not have the fight in us to say, *I will give it to so and so, as that work is assigned to them.* When work colleagues call on us on vacation days, we do not have the energy to say, *we are out of office.* We just don't have the juice. It's gone.

When you are in low-power mode, you don't have a lot of clarity. Let me repeat that: when you are tired, your brain goes into energy savings settings. It is easier when we are exhausted for our brains to choose the easiest, least resistant path. So we say yes. We answer the text. We answer the e-mail. We answer the question. We agree to the work. We unload the dishwasher ourselves even when someone else has been asked and said they would. We say yes to the party, the dinner, the volunteer event.

In 2018, I was exhausted with life. I found myself in a difficult conflict that was weighing on my mind every minute of every day. The energy it took to stay in the battle was more than I could bear at times. I couldn't see an easy way out. I had to remain strong and engaged in the battle, when all I wanted to do was escape. I remember talking to my friend, Aimee, one night.

"I am going to throw in the towel," I told her. "I think it is the right thing to do," I said, defeated. I couldn't stand up for myself anymore. I was completely worn out.

"You are war weary," she said. "You are NOT going to throw in the towel, you are going to take a break," Aimee said. She was absolutely right. I didn't need to concede; I needed to step away from the battle for a few days and decompress. I needed to sleep. I needed rest.

I took a few days away from the fight. I laid down my proverbial sword and rested. I eventually came out of that season of my life with some bruises, but more importantly, with a lifesaving awareness of how much fatigue and exhaustion affects my discernment. I almost backed down on my principles simply because I was tired. And guess what? This is a common weapon used on women. Wear us down, strike when we are tired, too tired to say no, too distracted to stand up for ourselves, too worn out to set boundaries.

Are you completely, chronically bone tired? If you are, you likely haven't had the energy and thus clarity to discern what boundaries are being crossed in your life and what boundaries you need to set.

Sleep, sister. Ask for help. Lay down all unnecessary tasks and ask others to help you do the ones that need to be done. Go to a hotel for a weekend—alone. I'm not kidding. Rest. Reset. Then pick up this book, and you'll be amazed at the energy you have to see what needs to go in your life and what needs to stay in the boundaries you've created.

6. We do not value ourselves enough to believe we have the right to set boundaries.

I saved the most difficult limiting belief for last. We may have a deep-seated belief that we haven't stopped to recognize, and we don't know how much damage it is causing to our well-being. The belief that your time or energy holds less value than another person's may be the reason you find yourself as a full-time people pleaser. Remember that, as young girls, we have been socialized to think our voice is not important, a seat at the table is less available, and our work is not worth as much salary as our male colleagues. Whether we recognize how the reality of being women in a male-dominated world affects our daily decisions, it permeates the foundation of our culture and has fingers in every institution and home.

We women are humans, and while we are different than our male counterparts, our differences make us uniquely suited to achieve success in amazing ways. Our value is in our humanity. I believe our worth doesn't come from some list of attributes someone tells us we must have but from simply being created as a child of God. We have every right as women to set boundaries, just as our male partners do, that are best for our health. We must ask ourselves, *Do we believe this?* When we find our voice faltering, when we cave to the desire to speak and push down our own needs or well-being at the expense of others, we must ask ourselves: *Do I really believe my time and energy are equal to that of others? Why or why not?* These are not easy questions, and they may lead you to uncomfortable thoughts and memories. But they are vital to your ability to overcome a boundary-less life and pursue work-life control.

Believing your value is innate and doesn't come from pleasing others takes effort. I still struggle at times with this belief myself, especially when a significant power differential exists with the person I feel I am indebted to please. I have to remind myself that speaking my true thoughts and setting boundaries furthers self-respect. People who respect and honor themselves, in the long run, are respected by others. I also remind myself that setting boundaries around my work allows me to focus on that work and over deliver. When I fail to set boundaries for work asked of me and take on more than I should take on, my work product suffers, whether that is at home or in the workplace.

Boundary Check-In

Let's review the six common limiting beliefs and reasons most of us struggle to set boundaries.

1. We don't recognize a boundary has been crossed.

2. We believe setting boundaries is "not our personality."

3. We believe it is easier to live boundary free.

4. We believe we have to say yes to everything.

5. We are too tired to set the boundary.

6. We do not value ourselves enough to believe we have the right to set boundaries.

Which one resonates the loudest with you?

Where did this belief or reasoning come from in your life story? In other words, why do you think you have adopted this belief?

What would happen if you stopped believing the false thought or were able to rest? How would time spent on your own well-being and priorities change things?

CHAPTER 5

JUST ADD BOUNDARIES

YOU DO NOT NEED MORE MOTIVATION OR CONFIDENCE. YOU NEED BOUNDARIES.

The only thing that separates a blessing from a curse is one's ability to enforce a boundary around it.

—Sasha K. Shillcutt

In 2009, we had just moved into our dream home. I was a young attending, trying to balance all the things in my career and home life. I had a six-year old, a four-year old, and an eighteen-month old. My life was pretty much coordinated chaos. So, of course, it was the perfect time for my husband to decide to get a dog. With the little energy I had left after working long hours in the operating room and wrestling three kids to bed each night, I resisted. Kind of. I mean, I tried.

One early Saturday morning, as I dragged my wearied self into the house after working twenty-four hours straight at the hospital, I met my husband Lance in the kitchen. He was prepping to load all three kids in the car. "Where are you going?" I asked.

"I thought I'd take them for a drive today and get out of the house so you can sleep," he replied. Looking back, that should have been my first clue.

Several hours later, he pulled into the driveway with a chubby, shy, sleeping English Labrador puppy and three exuberant, loud, shouting kids. Needless to say, Jack became a huge part of our hectic home life.

"I am not parenting this dog," I stated, after finding him face-deep in someone's Cheerios. "I am not disciplining this dog," I would say as I picked up chewed socks. You can imagine how well that went. I was angry at my husband for ignoring my boundaries, and we had several arguments. I don't want to give the impression that I am a stonewall, and no one ever crosses my boundaries. I am human, and my husband is human, and our boundaries differ. Sometimes concessions are made, and you meet in the middle. I saw how much my kids loved this dog, and I decided I would just set a boundary of having nothing to do with him.

Fast-forward a few months. After ruining multiple brand-new pieces of furniture by chewing through wooden bar stools, couch cushions, and end tables, I decided it was time I stepped in. Jack needed a mother.

I tried parenting him like I did my children. He rebelled. We hired Sally, the world's best dog trainer. "He needs to be kenneled, consistently," Sally said. I looked at her, perplexed. Sally went on to explain that he not only needed a kennel, Jack would grow to love it. Sally told me Jack needed a place to escape us, just like we needed time when he was not able to get into mischief. He needed to know his kennel was his space for sleeping and escape—not to chew toys, play, or eat—his haven away from the adults and children.

Sure enough, Sally was right. Within a few weeks, Jack could be found sleeping in his kennel with the door open. When we'd start to pack up to leave the house, we'd find him heading to his kennel. As I started to close up the house at night, he would trot to his kennel. When I would find something he had chewed up and call his name, he would drop his head and saunter sneakily to his kennel. It was essentially his room. As I type this, guess where Jack is? In his kennel. Twelve years later, he still loves his space.

A LESSON FROM JACK

Have you ever been in your house, your presumed safe place, and found yourself looking for an escape? If you are like me, and you have little people (or perhaps furry people) you are responsible for, there are times you just need to get away. Maybe your dream is to go to the bathroom by yourself. Maybe your dream is to enjoy a cup of coffee without someone asking you how to get nail polish out of the carpet. Maybe your dream is to eat a meal without your phone buzzing nonstop, requiring you to answer it.

So, after watching Jack basically teach me boundaries, in 2015 I decided I needed a kennel. Literally. I needed a place in my own home to escape, just like my English Lab did. I decide to make a nook in my bedroom, a small loveseat that I dubbed my decompression area. I went to Home Goods and bought a plush throw blanket, some cute throw pillows, and designated the nook my kid-free zone.

For the last seven years, I've spent at least fifteen minutes a day in this space. Everyone in my house knows that when I am sitting there, I am off the clock. I am usually reading, writing, thinking, and recharging. If you do not have this space in your home, you need one! It does not have to be a big space—it can be a chair or a small meditation bench in your closet! In my opinion, we all need a safe space that everyone knows signifies a time-out.

But here is the thing: My "mom space," by itself, has not provided a much-needed decompression space for daily-life stressors. It is the *boundaries* I set around this space that has given me a daily escape in my home when I need it. With his kennel, Jack basically has told us, "You humans cannot fit in here. Please stay out and respect my boundaries." I took a lesson from my pup. I had to teach the people I do life with that this space is my escape, and when I am sitting in it, they are not to bother me unless they are bleeding to death or are in severe danger. I wish my children would have the insight to say "Mom just worked fourteen hours and is sitting on her special loveseat having a moment. Perhaps I should ask her about math problems later," but I am telling you, sister, that is not the case. Unless I explicitly explain boundaries, they just don't happen. No matter how obviously exhausted, stressed, or tired I am, I have to communicate to others when I need a break, when I cannot help them, or when I simply need time alone. This is an example of how what I call *everyday boundaries,* or boundaries with those I share life with daily, have saved me.

Often, we get upset with others for not understanding or knowing our boundaries before we have explained them. But remember, a boundary is not a boundary if it is unspoken or quietly lives in your head. *A boundary only comes to life when it is communicated with others.* The truth is that we, as women, far more than men, need fierce boundaries. Why? Because men have built-in boundaries. Let me explain.

MYTH: If others really love us, they should know our boundaries without us having to tell them.

FACT: A boundary only comes to life when it is communicated with others.

If you have read *Between Grit and Grace,* my first book, then you likely know about what I call The Man-uel. It is the guidebook of how we as women are supposed to live, act, serve, and be all things to everyone in society. It is what I call the "not too much, but not too little" script of how women are expected to work, lead, and serve in order to stay within the margin of societal norms. If you have read *Between Grit and Grace,* then you also know that my answer to The Man-uel is to throw it in the trash.[xiv]

The thing about The Man-uel is that most women do not realize they are living their lives in an attempt to follow it, thereby setting themselves up for constant comparison and disappointment. They are not aware they trying to measure up to a definition of success that someone else has defined for them. Therefore, we as women often find ourselves on the hunt for the latest hack that will allow us to have a never-ending source of energy, a magic boost of confidence, or a secret trick that will create more hours in our day for us to do all the things for others. We are on a constant quest for self-improvement. We are convinced there must be something wrong with us. We are missing that thing, and if we could just find it, we would be able to be more, do more, serve more, and give more without feeling exhausted and defeated.

SELF-AGENCY

But here is the thing: Most of us do not need more confidence, attractiveness, skills, experience, or self-improvement. What we

need is self-agency, the belief that we, as women, as unique and different as each of us is, are really meant to define our own version
of success. Each of us is meant to take inventory of our unique talents and skillsets, abilities, and desires, and follow the path we were
meant to walk. As a spiritual person, I believe each of us has been
made uniquely by God to follow the path He has set for us, which
only we are meant to walk. We were meant to influence people in
ways only we, as individuals, can connect with; to lead and serve in
ways that bring us joy, even if it means not marching to the beat of
everyone else's drum.

To have self-agency, to truly ditch the expectations of others, we
as women do not need more confidence, money, power or likeability, we need boundaries. Live-saving, radical boundaries, that keep
our minds and bodies healthy, the expectations of others realistic,
and our individual definition of success in the forefront of our daily
activities and energy.

When you set boundaries, you reveal your authenticity. You
show others your priorities, which are completely different than
others', and that is okay. When you express your boundaries, that
is confidence. You become a confident person through the process.

You may be thinking you lack the confidence to set boundaries.
But the amazing thing is that confidence doesn't come from success,
but rather from taking action. Actions where we speak up for our
own health and well-being that result in self-confidence, independent of the outcome of the action. The mere act of setting boundaries, regardless of how insecure you feel in doing so, will result in you
leveling up. Each time you set a boundary with someone or around
an ask, you will feel a little more confident as you realize it is not
nearly as difficult as many of the things you have faced as a woman.

Confidence is like a muscle: the more you use it, the more you grow, even if working it out makes you extremely sore.

I got to know Dr. D. Bradley through one of the Brave Enough retreats, and I found her to be brilliant, hilarious, and authentic. Like most women I admire, her path has not been straightforward and easy. In fact, most of the gritty women whom I have gotten to know through my work have had to make hard decisions at some point or another and choose between likeability or well-being.

"One of the biggest lessons in boundary setting came after I was hired to what I thought was my dream job," Dr. Bradley said. "I very quickly realized the culture and leadership was toxic. I developed significant migraines and anxiety, and I was miserable. I didn't know how to quit; I felt like quitting would be failing. I finally had to place boundaries around my own mental well-being and made the decision that my mental health was more important than any job," she says. "Quitting that job was the best thing I could have done for myself, but it took me much longer than it should have because I was afraid to set the boundary," she explained. "I tried to convince myself I just needed to be someone different who could work in this culture. But the truth is, I was able to get a great new job where I am thriving. My confidence has increased significantly with setting boundaries. In order to set boundaries, I had to allow myself to be authentic, to stop people-pleasing and to make decisions based on what is healthiest for me. My negative self-talk, which zapped my energy and made me live with a fear of failing others, has decreased significantly, and as a result, my confidence has increased. I am becoming the CEO of my life," she states.

When you explain your boundaries to others, you become respected by those you want to keep in your circle. When you set boundaries, you fiercely protect your personal energy and health. You become closer to the person you were meant to be, and it feels lighter. When you set boundaries, you gain clarity and freedom. Why? Because you know that the people who respect you for your boundaries truly respect you for YOU. You can be free to be yourself around those people, unafraid of constant judgement or letting them down. You gain peace.

Learning to enforce boundaries in our lives allows us to grow in confidence. We become self-assured women when we trust ourselves to set boundaries and know we will be okay with any backlash that comes from doing so.

THE EGO DESPISES BOUNDARIES

In 2015, I began a small community online. It started with about thirty women. I added thirty women and told them they could each invite a friend. I truly thought the group would max out around fifty to seventy-five. I had no idea it would rapidly expand and grow into a network of thousands of women. By 2020, it had grown to nearly thirteen thousand women strong.

I loved this community like it was my fifth child. I nurtured it daily. The first year, I would go into the community each morning when I woke up and post something encouraging. Then, at night, I would check in and see what was going on. I would comment on nearly every woman's post in a way to support them. I felt responsible as the founder to nurture, protect, encourage, and inspire the women in the group. I spent about thirty minutes a day taking care of the community. By far the vast majority of the time I spent in the group was positive. It involved me encouraging, giving advice, answering questions, posting things to promote the women, and simply supporting women in the group.

As the community grew, so did the amount of time I found myself committing each day to moderate it. I started to receive direct messages from women in the group on a daily basis. Most of the time, the women had a question for me or something they were struggling with and needing advice. I felt that, as the leader of the group, it was my responsibility to respond to their requests. As I started to answer their appeals for help, the time I was spending on direct messages and giving advice started to grow. I would come home after a long day of work, rush to get the kids dinner and off to their activity, and then I would spend an hour or more before bed responding to my direct messages. My kids would ask me a question, and I would not hear them. My husband would interrupt me reading and texting responses, and I would snap at him, "I am in the middle of something important! This woman is facing (insert problem), and she really needs my advice; you have no idea what she is going through!" I would tell him.

It was overwhelming. It was also starting to affect my mental well-being, but I couldn't see it. Some of the things women were sharing were quite personal, and I would become upset reading some of the things they were going through. Some of the personal stories women shared angered me. Some of the stories grieved me beyond comprehension. There were common threads of gender bias. Discrimination. Domestic abuse. Gas lighting. Toxicity. Pay inequity. Divorce. Women being held back or overlooked for well-deserved promotions. Miscarriage. Infertility. Widowhood. Loss of a child. So much hardship. And grief.

I felt responsible to make space for all these women and the things they shared with me privately. Each morning, when I would open my phone, I would check my direct messages and pray. Often, I did not have the words to respond back to them. I started to create a list of women experts in law, mental health, gender bias, coaching, therapy, and women who privately helped women experiencing abuse create a plan of escape. I started referring women to these other women privately. At the same time, I found myself spending anywhere from fifteen minutes to one hour a day moderating the group to keep it a positive, safe place. It became a routine part of my life to spend time each day taking care of this free online community.

While I recruited several women volunteers to act as moderators to help me, the truth is that they didn't have the time (understandably so) to maintain the group. All but one of the moderators phased out, and even she, who hung with me the longest, burned out in attempting to keep the peace. While the group was free, I knew I needed to pay someone to maintain it, post announcements, add and review new members' requests, and administrate the group. I started paying an assistant to do this work, and I tried to focus on encouraging the women, nurturing the group, and making sure it served a positive purpose.

The group was a very positive source of light in my life. Like anything you care deeply about and pour energy into, it brought me great joy, while at the same time bringing me a lot of stress. But I couldn't think about or even contemplate not showing up every day for these women. I couldn't imagine turning off my direct messages, which were taking up a lot of brain space and a major amount of work each day to respond to. They were not *Hey, can you tell me where you bought your jeans?* type questions. These were long texts of women's stories of personal and professional hardship that I felt a responsibility to respond to.

Every time I would get exhausted or emotionally burned out, I would get down on myself for not being a strong enough leader to handle it. I would download a book on how to be a better leader and think, *Ok, I just need to scale myself!* When I would feel overwhelmed with the amount of time it was taking me to invest in the group, I would try to find even more people I could pay to help me. It was not only costing me money but costing me my relationships with my children and husband. My kids felt ignored, with good reason. I was constantly distracted on my phone. As I hired more people, I had to manage more people. It took more and more time.

I had tried on my own to turn off my direct messages, even a week at a time, but the backlash I would experience would overwhelm to me. I had enormous guilt when I would turn my notifications back on and read what I had missed. Women would write that they felt let down. I even posted an e-mail address so that women who felt they needed advice or help could e-mail. I paid an assistant to filter the e-mails. But this didn't' work either, as very few women followed the directions. Instead, they would continue to direct message. I was in over my head and desperate to figure out how to get this under control. I finally hired a business coach who could help me. When I began to tell her what I needed, she came down hard on my lack of boundaries.

"You need boundaries with your community," my coach, Alli, explained.

"Boundaries?" I whispered. I had felt shame even bringing up the fact that I could not handle the requests for help any more or being the peacemaker anymore. I felt weak, like a failed leader who would be letting everyone down if I tried to pull back in anyway.

"You need to stop pouring out your emotional strength and wisdom to strangers on the internet," she said bluntly.

Whoa. Her words hit me like a ton of bricks. I had not expected her to say this. I wanted her to give me some master schedule, some secret to creating more time in my day. I thought I would pay her to give me some elite coaching advice on how I could operate more efficiently. Maybe she knew some superpower that would allow me to create even more space for people who needed me in life.

"But I really like helping women," I explained. "I feel this is my gift, and I am not sure I can just stop," I went on to tell her. She told me that we needed a plan to take the work I was doing and put a name to it; then, put boundaries around it that would allow me to continue to help women, but in a healthy manner that would allow me to serve them and do it on the time I had set aside for it. She also explained that I could not continue to give away my time and energy for free and give my family my leftovers, which was exactly what I had been doing. I hung up the phone and wept. I realized I had taken a great thing like helping women and allowed it to evolve into a monster. A monster that was feeding my own ego on the false belief that "I have to help others," while allowing it to burn me out.

My complete lack of boundaries around this community had devolved from something that was special in my life, truly special to me, to something completely unhealthy. And no one was to blame for this but me—not the women who messaged me at all hours of the night, not the few women who created drama and projected their own issues on others in the community of vastly positive women, not the moderators who had left due to overwhelm, not my paid administrator who did her best to help me. No one, but me.

It was a hard reality to face, that I had allowed something beautiful in my life to become oppressive. But here's the thing: anything wonderful in life can become addictive, oppressive, or toxic if you let it. The only thing, and I mean the only thing, that keeps that from happening *is your ability to set boundaries around it.*

What boundaries represent, in many regards, is moderation. In this instance, I didn't want to stop helping women. I did not want to stop advising women, connecting women, and pointing them in the direction of healing and of stepping into their own power. I was really good at it, and it gave me JOY to see women break free from chains, toxic environments, discriminating bosses, and unhealthy workspaces. I loved seeing women create the work-life control they wanted, start spending time with themselves, and pursue their own definition of success. I had the ability and experience to help these women, and I didn't want to lose it. But I needed moderation. I needed radical, lifesaving boundaries. I needed brave boundaries that dared me to choose health over likeability, purpose over popularity.

My coach, Alli, and I mapped out how I could help women, but in a structured way that involved setting boundaries and clarity. It took me a few months, but what I created was now called Brave Balance, my masterclass for high-achieving women who find themselves burned out, overwhelmed, or stuck. Sound familiar? They say you create the content you need, and it is true. My direct messages became a controlled, happy place. Instead of causing me massive anxiety with every notification, I now had an answer. I had two options for women who needed help, one-on-one coaching or joining my coaching class. Until this point, I hadn't even realized that what I was doing was mentoring and coaching professional women. I was spending an hour before bed answering messages and giving advice, connecting women, helping women step through their pain points and break down limiting beliefs. I had become a coach, but

I had not realized that I could improve upon what I was doing. I developed a curriculum, brought women together in peer groups, and it exploded. Not only was this new way with boundaries much healthier for me, but it was actually deeper, more enriching, and more long-lasting than any messages or e-mail I could write at 11:00 PM I felt empowered. I felt authentic. I felt free. But mostly, I felt healthy. Gone was the guilt for not doing enough, the exhaustion of feeling like I couldn't help everyone, and the distraction of helping strangers at a cost to my own relationships and mental health. I realized that boundaries allowed me not only freedom but moderation. The boundaries I created around this community allowed me to keep something positive and beautiful from becoming something oppressive.

BOUNDARIES ARE LOVE

It is easy to hear the word *boundaries* and think they are restrictive and will cramp your style. But the truth is that boundaries are incredibly protective. They allow us to dive deep into our work, our family, our passion, in a healthy and moderate manner. We tend to cringe when we hear the saying "everything in moderation," but I promise you, it is true. If you think about the essence of love, the most precious commodity we have, at its truest form it is protected by brave boundaries. When love becomes oppressive, addicting, or overwhelming, it isn't love anymore. Even love, the richest object we can possess, is most valued when it is constrained.

If you think of the people who love you the most and whom you love the most, you likely have immense freedom and respect serious boundaries around that person. They are most likely the people in your life who you could hang up on when you are in the middle of something, and they would trust you to still love them and call them back when you can. They are the people who understand when you say you need a moment alone, or when you turn down their invite. They are the people who don't judge you for not being your best every day, but rather care most about your mental and physical health. They are the spouse who trusts your loyalty to them when you travel, because they love you the deepest.

One of my favorite scriptures is 1 Corinthians 13. It is commonly known as the love passage, and it lists an eloquent description of the attributes of love. My favorite verse is verse 9, which says: "[Love] always protects, always trusts, always hopes, always perseveres."[xv] I smile whenever I hear this verse read. To me, I interpret it to mean that love, in its truest form, protects. It isn't scared off by boundaries. It is protected by them.

Every day we make life choices based on many things. We hope our decisions are based on love, but many times they are based on our ego or the ego or needs of others. Sometimes we make decisions on how we spend our time and energy based on survival. If we are emotionally exhausted and physically burned out, our ability to maintain the energy it takes to enforce our boundaries falls to the wayside. And it can be very easy for us to confuse loving others, or loving ourselves as having no boundaries with a person. How many times do we hear someone describe a workaholic by saying they loved to work/lived to work. A person who has few professional boundaries does not love their work. They are likely using work to fill a void in their life and misinterpreting their lack of boundaries as a deep commitment or love for their profession.

Love isn't afraid of boundaries. It protects. It trusts.

The only thing that protects a beautiful aspect of your life from transforming into an unhealthy aspect of your life is your ability to enforce a boundary around it.

Let's dig deeper into this topic of boundaries around something in your life you love. Maybe it is a person. Maybe it is a project. Maybe it is your job, a hobby, or even a goal you have set for yourself you've fixated on for decades. Think of something in your life that you truly enjoy and love or that brings you immense pleasure, while simultaneously bringing you serious pain. When you think about it, you can't imagine how you can remove it from your life, but you also know you can't allow it to dominate and deplete you.

Boundary Check-In

1. Take a deep breath! You have the strength within you to unpack how you allow a person, project, task, or whatever it is to seep into your life and take control. You can and will be okay after you set boundaries around it. Perhaps it is not a person or work issue but a belief you have about yourself that dominates your everyday thinking. But you also enjoy whatever it is for it brings you some benefit. The first step is to identify that you need boundaries around it. Ask yourself this question: how can I show up for myself and align this issue/person/project with my priorities?

2. Write down all the positive things about this person/project/task that you want to keep. Make a list (simplify!) of three to five aspects of this area that you want to keep. For example, maybe you are a member of a volunteer organization. You love the people of the organization and the service aspect, but, unfortunately, they keep asking more and more of your time, and it has gotten to the point that, when you receive an e-mail from them,

you get a sick feeling in your stomach and ignore it. Because you haven't responded, the director has started texting you. You don't respond and feel terrible. Ugh. You have become "that person" who bails on those in need. So, you make a list. What is it that you want to do with this organization? You decide you want to donate money routinely and volunteer at their annual service event. Great. Remember that.

3. Write down three to five boundaries that would help you to moderate this person/project/task and keep him/her/it in your life without burning you out or exhausting you. For example, going back to the volunteer organization above, you could write: I will limit my communication to them by telling them my commitment for the year is one event and a monthly donation and explain that is what I have time for in my life this year. I will set up an automated withdrawal for a monthly donation so I don't forget to send it in.

4. Communicate the boundary with stakeholders. Not there yet? Practice writing down what you will say. Even if you do not feel like you have the strength to communicate your boundaries, just writing them down will feel empowering and allow you to think through your fears or your internal objections to be transparent about how you will move forward with this person, project, task, or issue. Remember, a boundary isn't a boundary until it is communicated. I routinely teach this to the women who take my courses. Step Four is, honestly, the hardest step, because we are so conditioned to do for others and keep showing up in a world that relies on women having no boundaries. But we can do hard things; we do them every day.

Living a life with brave boundaries is hard, but we choose our hard. Living a life with brave boundaries is also love. We do not need more confidence or to be liked by others. We do not need more Botox or self-improvement. We need radical, lifesaving brave boundaries, sister. The kind that require massive courage, honest self-reflection, and deep self-awareness.

So buckle up. Because in Chapter 6, we are about to get real, my friend. We are about to choose brave boundaries over our own comfort. And in doing so, we are about to choose freedom and love. Here we go.

CHAPTER 6

THIS MAY HURT A LITTLE

HOW TO IDENTIFY
WHAT BOUNDARIES YOU NEED

And it was not until I began to think,
that I began fully to know how wrecked I was,
and how the ship in which I had sailed was gone to pieces.[xvi]

—Charles Dickens

Most of the time we do not decide to make drastic changes in our lives until we have hit rock bottom. We do not decide it may be time to reign in our nightly ice cream when we gain one pound. We shrug it off and keep scooping mint chip until we can't fit into our favorite jeans. Then we decide to break the nightly sweets. We get asked to do an extra task at work for no pay, and we tell ourselves it will be a one-time thing. Until then, we are doing an hour or two of unpaid work each day, and we can't remember the last time we made it to the gym in the morning. Instead we are drowning in our to-do list and logging on an hour earlier just to keep up.

We don't make promises to ourselves to change our health or well-being when we are flying through life with zero problems and relentless energy. We don't modify our routines, improve our choices, or change our inner circle of people when things are comfortable and we are soaring. We don't decide we are going to sleep more and eat better, rest more and work less when we are feeling great. The truth is, for the vast majority of us, the only time we decide to make positive changes in our lives is when things are bad. Really, really bad.

So, if you are reading this and you can't remember the last time you washed your hair or put on real clothes, if you don't remember when you had more than four hours of uninterrupted sleep, this is a good thing. The timing of you reading this book is perfect. If you can't remember the last time you laughed or took an entire day to enjoy yourself, I am excited for you, because it likely means you are willing and ready to make brave changes in your life that will radically change your ability to live and breathe as *you*. In my work with high-achieving women, I can tell you that most of the time when they decide to sign up for my classes, it isn't because they are seamlessly juggling everything. They decide to invest in themselves and make changes because they have to, because they feel themselves losing control of their lives, cruising at 70 mph and careening off the shoulder hitting rumble strips. It is because they can't imagine continuing at the pace they're on or endure the stress level they are currently experiencing.

Welcome, sister. If this speaks to you, you are ready.

TAKING OUR BOUNDARY INVENTORY

In this chapter, we are going to take a boundary inventory. We are going to look at our lives from an outsider perspective and make a diagnosis. I am going to ask you to step on the scale, so to speak. We are going to run some tests and scan your life. It may be a little stress provoking, and it most definitely is going to be revealing. Before we dig in, I want you to assure you of this: no person on this planet has healthy boundaries in every area of their life. No one. Some of us have clear work boundaries. We have no problem leaving work where it belongs—at the office. But then we walk into our front door, and it's like the monkeys have taken hold of the shipwreck that is our home life, and we don't have the first clue how to gain back control.

Some of us have excellent boundaries with our family. But when our boss asks us to take work on our Italian vacation, we find ourselves saying, *Sure, no problem.*

The point is that all of us need help with boundaries in some part of our lives, and normally it is the area we don't want to think about. As we go through this next exercise, give massive grace to yourself as you honestly ask yourself the most important question: *Why do I lack boundaries in this area?*

First, let's remember that our thoughts create our feelings, and our feelings drive our actions. If our thoughts are "we must please others," then our ego is fed from doing so, which makes us crave more people-pleasing and leads to a dangerous cycle that ends in burnout. Everything starts with our thoughts, and that is why it is so important to go back to them before we try to go forward.

The why behind your lack of boundaries in this area may not be fun to uncover. I get it. I have been there. But it is so important to discover why you think you can't set healthy boundaries for yourself. Chances are that you don't realize there may be an actual reason you are avoiding setting them, beyond pure exhaustion and your never-ending to-do list or the fact you can't even pee in your home by yourself without interruption. Table 1 lists some common reasons we may lack boundaries.

Reasons you may lack boundaries:
The feeling of being needed feeds your ego.
You fear disappointing the person/group.
You tried to set a similar boundary before and failed.
You don't think you are strong enough to set the boundary.
You believe you won't be loved if you set the boundary.
You don't believe you deserve to live with the boundary.
You didn't realize you actually needed a boundary.
Pleasing people feeds your ego.

TABLE 1.

A few months after the COVID-19 pandemic hit and it became clear it was here to stay, I remember feeling this deep wave of grief and overwhelm. I approached the pandemic like most challenges in my life: *I will conquer this!* I thought. *I will be victorious. I will take care of myself, my family, my patients, my clients, and WILL COME OUT SHINING!* were my classic internal thoughts on repeat. There was no way I was going to crumble to this virus that decided to take hope, people's livelihoods, people's lives, their plans, vacations, events, and relationships. Not on my watch! I was going to conquer this thing.

You can laugh at me, but this is how I approach most things. My personality, when presented with difficulties and problems, is that I take it on as a challenge to my resilience. My initial reaction to disappointment and crises is very much, *Try me.* So, when the pandemic initially hit and fear was prevalent, I went into fight mode: *Just try me, COVID-19.* Come and get me. I adopted internal mantras such as, *I will make it to vaccination! I will not falter!* Mask up? *No problem, nasty virus. I've been wearing a mask for twelve to twenty-four hours at a time for seventeen years as an anesthesiologist. Stay at home and school people? No problem. I was homeschooled for part of my schooling growing up. I am on it!*

I know, I know. It is ridiculous and wrong to think you can control your likelihood of avoiding a virus, but man did I try. I didn't want some virus to steal my forward progress and joy. And I took it on as a personal challenge to care for and protect my people like I had never done before. I started doing things I would normally do as a treat for my family every day. I started cleaning their rooms. Cooking major meals. Making homemade treats. Doing things to make their lives easier. I felt totally responsible for the well-being and happiness of my people. It became somewhat an obsession to make sure everyone was happy and okay.

But the truth was that my people were not all happy and okay. Like most of the world, we were living in a pandemic. There were ongoing cancelations, illnesses, mountains of stress, and unknowns. There was isolation, virtual learning, and canceled sport seasons, proms, and recitals. All the while, as the hope started to fade, I kept trying to make everyone happy. The more it didn't work, the harder I tried.

About six months into the pandemic, I crashed. I could barely function after long days in the operating room and facing my family at night. I was struggling to keep up with the demands of my online community. I was having anxiety that I wasn't doing enough and that I was letting everyone down. I could barely open my phone without instantly feeling uneasy. I dreaded logging on to any social media platform, as there was so much unrest and conflict. I found myself spending more and more time trying to keep the peace with others in my home and in my online community. I assume I was experiencing what most working moms were facing: trying to show up for work and give my all, check in with my loved ones and make sure my kids were mentally okay, do all I could to keep my elderly parents and in-laws healthy and safe from the virus, then crash and do it all over again the next day.

In order to set boundaries, there are two main things you need to possess:

1. The awareness that a boundary is needed

2. The energy to enforce it

So here I was, this woman who by all means was supposed to have her work-life balance figured out. After all, I was an accomplished author, physician, mom, and leader. I could not have achieved the success I have had working in a male-dominated environment without boundaries. And yet, if you asked me in the fall of 2020 how I was doing, I likely would have responded, "I am great!" until I climbed into my car after work and cried myself home. And most nights I struggled to tell myself, *You do not need a glass of wine, Sasha.* I found myself drinking more wine, feeling less at peace, and feeling overall exhausted.

It took me a while to realize that I had let massive boundaries slip. The person I needed the most boundaries with was . . . myself. I had this overwhelming desire to protect everyone, encourage everyone, help everyone, and respond to everyone. And instead of reeling in my desire to help everyone in view, when I became fatigued, I just tried harder.

I share this story because, while there were some areas in my life where I had developed very strong boundaries (such as doing unpaid work, speaking for no pay, work interruptions, and responding to e-mail), there were other areas where I had zero boundaries. It was not until I put my biggest pain point into the context of boundaries that I realized I could develop a plan to get my life back under control.

THE BRAVE BOUNDARY MODEL

I call this our Brave Boundary Model. The Brave Boundary Model is how we are going to identify if the problem you are experiencing is an area of your life that can be improved if you identify and enforce a boundary. Not every single challenge or problem you have in your life is a result of lacking boundaries. Think car accidents, betrayal, losing your keys, or cancer, for example—these are not things you can really improve with boundaries, but many areas are. I tend to be a believer in focusing on the things you can control and asking God to give you the strength to navigate the rest. Boundaries are something any of us can create and implement, which is fantastic news when you are tired, exhausted. and done in.

So let's go through the Brave Boundary Model. It is simple and easy because it is how I do life. It is not some complex, useless equation I'm asking you to memorize like the Krebs cycle or the quadratic formula. It is based on a few targeted questions I ask myself when I get to the end of myself and find myself angry, in tears, and completely frustrated, lying in a heap on my closet floor. The Brave Boundary Model is what I normally find myself contemplating when I am angry and frustrated with either myself or another person for a reason(s) I can't put my finger on. Typically, the light bulb only goes off when I start to work the model, and I am hopeful it will for you too. The Brave Boundary Model has four pertinent questions you ask yourself to decide if a boundary is needed. It's like a funnel. It's brave because self-reflection in the middle of chaos when you are energy depleted requires *courage*. Let's facc it. It is much easier to ask yourself, *what can make me feel better now?* It is less tiring to grab a glass of wine and attempt to numb the stress of the day than to stop and ask yourself, *what will make me feel better tomorrow, and the day after?*

The first and most important question of the Brave Boundary Model is this: *what do I know to be true?* I promise you, it may seem like a very basic question but it is the single most important step in identifying and enforcing a boundary. It takes all the fuzzy, angry, exhausted, confused emotions and uncomplicates them. It removes all the gray haze from your acute stress—which can billow up as if something just blew up around you—and allows you to get laser-focused on the sources of your problem. Why is this important? Because it *allows you to become laser-focused on the answer.*

To explain what I mean, I'm going to use the Brave Boundary Model on a problem I seem to have on the regular: my cell phone. On a typical day, let's say I finish my workday in the operating room around 5:00 PM. No one at work is aware that I plan on meeting my family at seven o'clock this evening to watch my son play soccer. I have about an hour of e-mails to answer at the hospital, and about thirty minutes of *Brave Enough* team updates and check in with my team, which leaves me thirty minutes to get to my family commitment. Everything is looking good for my plan. I rush from the operating room to my office to change out of scrubs. I log in to my desktop and fly through e-mails. While I am doing this, my phone starts exploding. I receive a text from a friend whom I haven't heard from in a while.

"Are you okay?" I read.

"I am good, why?" I quickly text back. She starts texting me that I'm receiving negative feedback online. I am unaware, as I have blocked or unfriended these individuals. All of a sudden, my amygdala has been hijacked. I get a terrible feeling in my gut. I start to feel flushed and tachycardic. My mind starts to go into anxiety mode, and I feel paralyzed for a minute. My plan to knock out e-mails is derailed. What should I do?

All of the sudden, my brain floods my consciousness with the thoughts: *I have upset someone; I've done something wrong; I am a bad person; I am under attack.* My fight or flight is in full on ten mode. Shame. Stress. Fear. Paralysis. In an instant, I go from knocking out working in my office and getting to my son's soccer game to feeling anxious, stressed, ashamed, and sad.

It takes no time at all for my actions to follow my thoughts. I stop all work. I start searching online, asking my friend for more information. I text my staff member who handles social media. I explain what is going on. I feel sick to my stomach as my parasympathetics are battling my sympathetic nervous system. I have no idea what I have done to cause the haters to come out today, but they have. Apparently, someone in a social media group I am not in suggested me as a speaker, and some women who aren't Sasha fans decided to go on the war path. The results equaled drama in the group.

I do what I can (which really is nothing when you are attacked online) and drive to my son's game. I am late. I am sad. I am stressed. I am unfocused. I am physically present, but I am not *truly engaged*. I give a half-smile to my youngest son who runs to me, excited to see me. I think I'm good at hiding my stress, but the truth is that within thirty seconds of my arrival, my family can see I'm upset. I spend the entire hour and a half trying not to look at my phone, but I fail multiple times. Every time I look for a new message, my stomach lurches a little. I don't really enjoy the game, my family is quiet, and I am frustrated that my night is ruined.

Brave Boundary Model
1. What do I know to be **TRUE**?
2. What can I **CONTROL**?
3. How can I set a **BOUNDARY**?
4. Whom do I need to **SHARE** it with?

TABLE 2 THE BRAVE BOUNDARY MODEL.

As I wash my face to get ready for bed, it hits me. This entire night was hijacked because I allowed a boundary to be crossed in my personal time. By engaging with gossip over a text message, I let complete strangers online derail my night, encroach on my family time, cause me to experience anxiety, and negatively affect my health. I decide it is time to use the Brave Boundary Model (Table

2) and get my mind settled before I go to bed and anxiety robs me of much needed sleep.

Here we go:

What do I know to be true? I ask myself as I crawl into bed. The truth is that some people were criticizing me in a social media group. That's it. That is all I know to be true. There are people who don't like me. Is this news to me? Not really. Then why did it upset me? Because I started to assign all these other meanings to the fact some people don't like me. Such as: *I did something wrong, I am a horrible human, or I should be more of something I am not.*

Aha, I found it. Those statements are not true. Once I identified the false beliefs my mind started to formulate, I pressed on and decided to ask myself the second question.

What can I control? The second question of the Brave Boundary Model is important, because it allows you to assume power over the situation and allows you to breathe for a minute. The truth is, in my situation described above, I could have kindly told my friend that I wasn't interested in hearing about the negative comments towards me. I could have stopped my inquisitive mind and told her, for my own mental health, that it wouldn't serve me to know any more about it. I could have stopped the information from crossing a mental health boundary I had set for myself several months prior that allowed me to free myself from having to be in the know about every negative comment or gossip other people decided to fling at me online, in text groups, or in comments behind closed doors. As someone wise once said, "What other people think about you, is none of your business." The truth is, even if I had zero social media presence and wasn't brave enough to share online my thoughts and beliefs, there would be people in this world who wouldn't like me. You may have a zero online presence, but the truth is there are people who don't like you, don't agree with you, and have decided in their own minds you aren't "their kind of people."

None of us can control how other people react to us. We can do our best to treat others with respect, be authentic, and truly be people who reach across the divide and someone will still reject us for who we are.

The sooner you stop allowing other people to measure your worth, the sooner you feel confident and in the driver's seat of your own personal peace.

This led me to ask myself the third question to the Brave Boundary Model: *How can I set* (or in this instance, reset) *a boundary?* The boundary I needed to reset was allowing others to share negative criticism or comments with me that were at me, but not for me. Let me explain.

I have set a very clear boundary for my mental health that involves criticism. I have to do this because even if the truth is criticism, when shared with you by people who have your best interest in mind, it is a gift. However, criticism or negative feedback shared with you by those whose primary goal is to stir up drama, to make you feel badly about yourself, or project their own insecurities onto you can be devasting and unhealthy. It is important that we establish a criticism boundary.

There are times in my life when I can handle criticism from those who care about me. The delivery is timely, I know the person is an ally, and I know the feedback they are giving me will only serve to make me a better person. We all have blind spots; it is our closest friends and colleagues who often are most aware of our near-sightedness or weaknesses that we need to redirect or bring to awareness. While no criticism is fun to hear, I start by asking myself, "What is the intent?" For example, if I know that my boss wants me to succeed, when he tells me how to improve my communication with a group of people, I listen. Do I feel great when he gives me criticism? No. But, I also don't feel bad about myself, because I know he truly wants me to succeed, and there is no shame in not being a perfect employee. However, when a work colleague who is constantly competing with me and throwing me under the bus at every opportunity gives me the same feedback and suggestion, I am not going to listen. I don't trust the source or the intention. The criticism may be valid; but what I have learned in life is that if you are a person who is open to feedback, the right people at the right time will deliver it to you. I ignore the rest.

So in this case, I was listening to and letting my brain too deeply indulge in criticism by people online whose only intention was to fling their own insecurities onto me; I was not living my own boundary. The truth is that the lack of following my own boundary didn't just have consequences for my own health, it had negative consequences for my entire family. How many times have you let someone who does not have your best interest in mind steal your happiness and affect your relationship with your loved ones? How many times have you allowed a comment or e-mail by a work colleague derail your day, and you then blamed that person? How many times have you allowed someone else's drama to stop you from completing work you needed to get done so that you can have family time or time for self-care? The beauty of the Brave Boundary Model is that we can learn from these scenarios and prevent them from happening again.

So, I asked myself the final question of the Brave Boundary Model, because I wanted to STOP the mental torture, the anxiety, and the loss of sleep.

Whom do I need to share the boundary with? Here is the thing: *Most of the time we need to share the boundary with ourselves. Over and over.* How many times had I told myself that *I am not going to accept worthless, negative criticism and online attacks by people not in my arena?* The truth is, many times. And yet, in this moment of rushing at the end of my day, I caved. I let the boundary be crossed, by me. I allowed myself to hear gossip and be sucked into the drama created by insecure people. I forgave myself in the moment and said to myself "Tomorrow is a new day to enforce healthy boundaries."

I also needed to set the boundary with my friend. The next morning, I sent her a text. I told her that I had given it thought, and the gossip and negative information she shared with me was detrimental to my mental health. I told her the next time she read or saw negative comments about me, the best thing to do was to not tell or pass it along to me, unless she thought it was from a source that had my best interest in mind, or she thought I was being attacked for things that could be detrimental to my professional reputation and required legal action. She apologized for telling me and was completely supportive. In fact, not only has she stayed steadfast to her promise, she has also defended me online by telling others I don't indulge or care about such comments. She is a true friend.

To summarize, the Brave Boundary Model involves asking yourself these four questions:

1. What do I know to be **TRUE?**

Remove the speculation, drama, and false beliefs.

2. What can I **CONTROL?**

This stops you from embracing victim mode and puts you in control!

3. How can I set a **BOUNDARY?**

Taking action empowers us.

4. Whom do I need to **SHARE** the boundary with?

A boundary shared is a boundary enforced.

Hopefully by now, you have identified an area of your life that requires a boundary or two.

There are several different areas of our daily lives that need clear boundaries. If you are still unclear on this, as I have directed you before, *think of the largest pain point in your life and start there.* Bring that scenario to your mind as we discuss the different categories of boundaries that are often needed. Listed below in Table 3 is a list of common boundaries that we may struggle with. Remember, as you think about what boundaries you need, give yourself grace. Resist the urge to compare yourself with your spouse, a coworker, or your best friend. The boundaries you may struggle to create are likely easy for someone else in your life to enforce, and vice versa. Grace, sister, grace!

BOUNDARY CATEGORIES

Here are some common areas where we may find ourselves lacking any kind of boundary. In fact, the chances are we have never even thought of this area of our lives as needing boundaries. That is okay! The entire purpose of *Brave Boundaries* is to help you identify new boundaries and reinforce old ones. If you go with me on this journey, by the end of this book, you will be what I call a *boundary rebel*. (Um, yes. Sign me up! Who wants a t-shirt?)

Boundary Category	Example
Family boundaries	• Family member communications, visits, vacations, holidays, interruptions, crisis managements • Family members with mental illness, disruptive or dysfunctional relationships, or those who trigger unhealthy behaviors • Children: interruptions, sleep, physical space (*i.e.*, bedroom, office spaces that are off-limits without permission) • Domestic duties and tasks
Professional boundaries	• E-mail • Text/calls during nonwork times • Vacation/out-of-office boundaries • Accepting/doing unpaid work • Coworkers who interrupt, elicit work drama • Office time/closed door
Personal boundaries	• Exercise/physical health • Romantic relationships/marriage • Friendships • Social events • Volunteer organizations
Electronic boundaries	• E-mail • Text/phone calls • Social media • News/television
Emotional boundaries	• Body Image • Past failures rehash and replay • Difficult coworkers, colleagues, and friends • People-pleasing

TABLE 3. THE DIFFERENT CATEGORIES OF BOUNDARIES AND EXAMPLES OF EACH

These are just a few broad categories that require us to set boundaries. This list is not meant to overwhelm you or urge you to go on full freak-out mode and throw this book across the room. None of us have perfect boundaries! Even Oprah has devoted episodes of her show and her Soul Sunday podcast to the importance of setting boundaries. "You have *to be able to set* boundaries, otherwise the rest of the world is telling you who you are and what you should be doing. You can still be a nice person and set boundaries," Winfrey said on *The Oprah Show.* "It feels great to be connected to people, but having boundaries is so important."[xvii] Oprah explained that she was forty-two-years old before she learned to set boundaries. If the queen herself learned this in her fourth decade, it is not too late for us.

Boundary Check-In

1. When you look at the list of categories, what is one example of a boundary that jumps out at you? Write it down.

2. Using the Brave Boundary Model, go through each question to work the model on the boundary you selected in Question 1. Resist the urge to become overwhelmed with the questions and answer each with the first thing that comes to mind. How does working the boundary make you feel? Less or more anxious? Less or more empowered?

3. When you think of the last question in the Brave Boundary Model, who comes to mind that you need to share your boundary with? Yourself? Another person?

4. Think of the person with whom you need to share the boundary. Set a time to speak to them this week. Practice talking it out with a friend. Think of

how you will feel, and write down your worries. Ask yourself: What is the WORST thing that could happen? What is the BEST response that could happen?

Remember: you cannot control how others will respond or react to your boundaries. Your responsibility is to set the boundary. Chances are, you will gain the other person's respect by doing so, and they will understand your boundary in time. If they don't respect your personal or professional boundary, it will reinforce how very much you needed the boundary in the first place.

Feeling empowered yet? Keep going! Get excited for the next chapter, as we will reinforce where to begin to truly become boundary rebels and set boundaries in all the major aspects of our lives . . . to take back control!

CHAPTER 7

DIGGING FENCE POSTS

HOW TO BEGIN TO SET BOUNDARIES

You get what you tolerate.[xviii]

—Henry Cloud

Now that we have identified what areas in our life would benefit from brave boundaries, we are going to learn how to set them. Setting boundaries takes immense courage. This is not easy work, and I am very serious when I say you are courageous for making it this far. It takes massive energy to set boundaries, and it is counterculture to do so, especially as a woman. I cannot talk about how to set boundaries without first telling you the truth: it is not a walk in the park. It is unnatural for most of us, it is quite difficult for women, and when you start to do it, you will receive backlash. I do not tell you this to scare you off; I tell you this because this is not some self-help fluff book that tells you to just *manifest the boundary, and it will* *be there.* I'm not suggesting you just believe in the boundary, and it will be there to the tune of *throw it into the universe and peace will come back to you!*

I am a physician, a mother of four, a tenured professor, and a gender-equity researcher. I have worked long enough in a male-dominated world to understand the complexities and realities of being a woman with boundaries. It is, for all intents and purposes, a battlefield. The world does not love women who set boundaries; it does not know what to do with women who exhibit the courage to protect their mental and physical health by setting boundaries. Men and women alike are threatened by women who believe their well-being is just as important as another person's agenda. I call these women boundary rebels. Setting boundaries is so counterculture, once you start it, you are rebelling against the status quo.

BECOMING A BOUNDARY REBEL

So, if you think I am going to ask you to chant some affirmations and the world will suddenly bring people into your life that respect and love the new you with boundaries, think again. This is difficult work, deep work, brave work, courageous work. It is work I believe in, and it is work I am confident any person can do. You can be courageous and set brave boundaries. I do not know a person who lived through 2020 who was not forced to find more strength than they thought they had and did so with grit and grace.

If the authority of women was normalized and respected, setting boundaries would be easy and everyone would do it.

Let's say you don't believe me when I say that setting boundaries is counterculture and requires significant courage. Perhaps you are reading this and thinking *it cannot be that hard or abnormal. What is wrong with women? Just set the boundary; it will be fine!* As a gender equity researcher, I invite you to look at this in the context of hard data.

THE STATUS OF WOMEN IN THE WORKFORCE

According to the US Department of Labor, in 2017 there were 74.6 million women in the civilian labor force, comprising 56.8 percent of all workers. Yet, while the Department for Professional Employees notes that half (51.5 percent) of employed women work in management-level positions and/or professional roles, only 4.4 percent of the CEO positions within the S&P 500 Companies are held by women. Sadly, in 2020, due to the COVID-19 pandemic, these statistics significantly worsened. According to the Center for American Progress, four times as many women have been furloughed during 2020 as men, with approximately 865,000 women dropping out of the US workforce in 2020.[xix]

Before you start thinking *women aren't as educated or qualified for these leadership roles when compared to men,* think again. According to US labor statistics, more women than men have earned bachelor's degrees by age twenty-nine (34 percent of women compared to 26 percent for men), showing an ambition for better employment opportunities.[xx] After age thirty-four, women earn advanced degrees at nearly the same rate as men (10.2 percent for women, 10.9 percent for men). One of the thorniest and most obvious issues is at every level of employment is the reality that women face discrimination in pay. According to the Institute for Women's Policy Research (IWPR), the median annual earnings gender wage-gap for full-time, year-round workers is 18.5 percent.[xxi] The truth is that we are educated, and we are doing several aspects of our jobs for free. What this tells me is that *women lack boundaries and face backlash when they enforce them.*

The reality is that when women decide to say *no more* and set boundaries, we often do so by displaying *agentic* traits. The word *agentic* is derived from the word *agency,* which, according to Merriam Webster, means, "the capacity, condition, or state of acting or of exerting power."[xxii] Stereotypically, agentic traits are associated with men—words like strong, authoritative, powerful, intelligent, and determined. The opposite of agentic is the word *communal,* which is stereotypically used to describe more feminine, or female attributes that our society comfortably associates with women—words like sensitive, caring, compassionate, and understanding.

Why is this important? Because when we think of the word *boundary* or the act of setting a boundary, our brains may instantly think that setting a boundary means speaking up and telling others what we will tolerate, or what is most healthy for us—agentic traits. Many times, when we think of times we have defended our own well-being, mental health, have told others we do not work for free, or say no to an invite, we realize we have faced backlash. When we act as our own agent, the world collectively gasps. Everyone pauses and stares at one another, and we may even experience a negative retort or reply. Why? Because the world does not see boundary setting as a communal trait but as agentic. And we know that women who adopt agentic traits in certain scenarios make everyone feel uncomfortable. Setting boundaries can be awkward, especially for the woman setting the boundary, and requires immense courage. We often receive backlash, and research tells us that women who act in their own agency are often perceived by their peers as unlikeable.

Research published by Williams and Tiedens showed that when women advocate for themselves, they are more likely to receive lower likeability scores than when their male counterparts to do the same.[xxiii] How many times have you heard in connection with a woman who is strong or more direct in her communication, *"You know, she's pretty blunt, but I still like her!"* or *"I don't mind her directness, that is just how she is."* We often refer to women who speak with authority, or women who adopt agentic traits, as having a character flaw that we must overlook, and we pat ourselves on the back when we decide to like them anyway. We are conditioned to think that being authoritative, speaking up, exerting our expertise is a *problematic attribute* as a woman, which we can look past it, for we are such admirable people. I challenge you to ask yourself: when have you ever heard this same discussion or comments about men? Likely, you haven't. Our gender stereotypes run deep. None of us, regardless of gender, can operate in our world free of bias.

STEREOTYPE THREAT AND BOUNDARY BACKLASH

One problem with stereotypes is that they can lead to something called *stereotype threat*.[xxiv] Research has shown that when we are aware of negative stereotypes, the stereotype itself can affect and predict negative outcomes in our actions.

Here is an example. Researchers divided a group of female college students into two groups. Prior to administering a test, they asked one group if they were good or bad at math. The other group was simply given the test. They found that the group asked if they were good or bad at math scored lower than the group not asked any questions about math ability.[xxi] In other words, when the female students were subtly reminded of the stereotype that women are not as good at math, it affected their test performance. It affected the way they perceived their own abilities, and it *affected their actions.*

This is important because there is a reason that we women do not set boundaries as easily as men. It is not because we are less intelligent. It is because it is not acceptable to say no to others' asks if you are a woman in our society. The stereotype of being a woman who has no problems setting boundaries means accepting a lot of negative backlash and may even affect the way we perform. Our ability to perform and produce may be worsened when we are working and living in environments where we may be experiencing sexism and misogyny on a daily basis.

For example, let's examine a study of women engineers by Logel and colleagues.[xxv] The researchers found that women engineers who worked in environments where the researchers had men act and engage in sexist behavior—for example, they had men make comments that women weren't as smart as their male colleagues—performed lower on tests than women engineers who didn't experience the same sexism. In other words, our environment matters. We start to experience what is called "social identity threat," where who we are as people is devalued, and we, in fact, start to believe it about ourselves. It affects our confidence, our behavior, and our ability to perform to the best of our ability.

I don't know about you, but I do not have to think far into my work history to recall a time when I allowed other people's opinions of me and my skills to affect my performance. As an anesthesiologist, I work in a unique environment in medicine. Every day my skills and ability to practice as an expert are reviewed in real time by one of my peers: namely, the surgeon. While I am intubating, placing invasive monitoring, performing procedures, making clinical decisions, etc., the surgeon is watching me. And vice versa. While the surgeon is cutting and sewing, I am watching. Surgeons and anesthesiologists are unique this way; in no other specialty in medicine are two physicians working in concert on the same patient, at the same time, in front of their peers.

Ninety-nine percent of the time, we support one another. In my practice, I work with cardiothoracic surgeons whom I count as friends. I watch my surgical colleagues do incredibly difficult procedures with skill and precision. It is not easy. And many times, there are difficulties and complications that are unavoidable. And the same goes for me. There are times I have difficulty completing a procedure, and they are watching me. Most of the time, they are encouraging me or giving me advice. They trust me as an expert, and I trust them, so I welcome it. But this has not always been the case.

When I was more junior in my practice, I didn't always work with the same group of collegial surgeons. Our practice was more random, and I would often have to work with surgeons I may only do cases with once a month or less. There was one particular surgeon who would stand over me, arms crossed, when I would do a procedure. I remember one harrowing night, a difficult case that I was trying to get lifesaving access on a patient who was dying. No one could get an intravenous access, and we couldn't treat him or proceed with the procedure until someone did. That someone was me.

As the patient was dying, alarms ringing, the entire team was watching me struggle. I was trying to get access through a tiny vessel, and every attempt would only cause more bleeding. The surgeon, instead of offering words of encouragement or help, started to yell at me. "You don't know what you are doing!" he screamed. My hands were shaking. The patient was dying. And the truth was that no one in the room was more qualified than I to do the procedure. Frustrated at me, he turned to the operating room nurse and screamed, "Get someone in here who knows what the hell they are doing!" She looked at me with huge eyes, stressed. She knew what I knew: the surgeon wanted a replacement for me, and I was the best shot this patient had. The nurse could call for help, but I was the person who would be called. She gave me a painful look as she started to call another anesthesiologist with less experience than I to come and help under the surgeon's direction.

I kept working and eventually got venous access, and the case proceeded. But not without me being incredibly traumatized by the event. My confidence was shattered. I started the "shouldas." You know, the internal dialogue you begin with yourself when you underperform, fail, or make a mistake. *I should have gotten access sooner,* I would think to myself. *I should be a better anesthesiologist than I am,* I would whisper internally. Whenever I would run in to members of the OR team who were on the case that night, I would avert my eyes as I passed them in the hallway. I felt shame—like I had somehow not been as good as I should have been and the surgeon's disparaging remarks were true.

The problem was that I had many other experiences with this same surgeon over the next several years. While I didn't work with him every day or even every week, when I did, I dreaded it. My hands would shake. I would second-guess clinical decisions I made, afraid I was making the wrong ones. I would question my own abilities, something I would never do had I been with a different surgeon. I would hesitate on making decisions and not speak up as authoritatively as I normally would. Basically, I would underperform. I didn't trust myself. It took me several years and some debriefing, but now

I look back and see how his inappropriate behavior, his ego, and his misogyny *was on him.* It was his problem, not mine. I let his opinion and his stereotypical behavior threaten my ability to perform. It was a classic case of stereotypical threat and social identity threat.

I learned some affirming things to do to offset his behavior. I would do breathing exercises for one to two minutes prior to entering the operating room with him. I would ignore him completely by picturing him as a toddler throwing a fit. I had toddlers at home. I knew how to deal with them. So that is how I dealt with him. I got to the point where I had to stifle a giggle when he would start in. And you know what? I was confident of my ability to perform, and I did. But it took me several years to be able to get there.

DIGGING FENCE POSTS

How did I do this? I used the *Brave Boundary Model.* While several of my peers dreaded their days in the operating room with this surgeon, I learned to set a boundary, go about my business, and not let him ruin my day. Here's what my Brave Boundary Model looked like:

1. What do I know to be **TRUE?**

   This surgeon is unhappy and speaks to me in a way that I don't prefer.

2. What can I **CONTROL?**

   I can control my response and attitude, and my ability to perform.

3. How can I set a **BOUNDARY?**

   I will not respond to the surgeon's yelling, threats, or anger. I will speak calmly and act unaffected. I will

continue to do my job well. If he starts in, I will ask
him to leave the OR while I do my work if he can't
keep his emotions in check.

4. Whom do I need to **SHARE** the boundary with?

I will share the boundary with the OR team if he
starts to be inappropriate again.

Guess what? It worked! It turns out that when you stay calm and point out when a person is being inappropriate, but you are unaffected by it and are going to do your job, they realize they cannot bully you. They retreat. And if they don't, and it escalates, then guess what? Everyone in the room gets uncomfortable, and you can call for help. When you remain calm, the margin between your calm and the other person's anger widens, and so does the ability to document their behavior and escalate it to the proper channels.

The more someone resists your boundary, the more it reveals your need for it.

I call this digging fence posts. Looking back, I am grateful I had this experience early in my career. It made me evaluate how I would let others treat me. It made me recognize I needed to dig a fence post and place clear lines on how I was going to allow others to speak to me, intimidate me, respect me. It would be great if we lived in a world where every person we encountered treated us with respect and dignity, and no one was ever under stress or duress, acting out their worst behavior, but the truth is, we don't. The truth is that I had no idea what was happening in that surgeon's life. I had no idea what his thoughts were about me or women anesthesiologists. And while I am not making excuses, I am pointing out that we cannot fix people or change their behavior. We can, however, set boundaries, communicate those boundaries, and stick to what we know to be true.

I had to learn to dig fence posts in many areas in my professional life. The next time a surgeon snapped at me, I was ready. I smiled and ignored him, and then said, "I am working on doing 'X' right now. If you are going to speak to me in that voice, I will ask you to leave the OR until I am done, and then I will be happy to speak to you at the scrub sink." While 99 percent of the time I never need to say this, I know it's in my arsenal, and I can set the boundary easily with any surgeon. And you know what? Most of the time, when this rarely happens, the surgeon apologizes. Maybe not right then but later. I've had many surgeons stop me the next day or call me later and apologize for their words while explaining the stress they are under. The truth is, we never know what is going on in a person's life. Many times, if you respond firmly but kindly, you give the person both space and grace. Chances are, there will be times when the tables will be turned (as has been the case with me several times), and you will need the same grace and space from them.

Power differentials can muddy boundary lines, and we may find ourselves feeling unable to set boundaries around those in power over us. These are tricky situations. Sometimes our jobs may even be at risk, or the backlash we may face for setting boundaries with those who determine our position and pay may have serious consequences that extend beyond ourselves. In these situations, I stick to three truths: (1) any boundary that protects one's ethics is one worth setting; (2) setting boundaries with those in higher positions requires allies in higher positions; and (3) take time to ask for advice before setting these kinds of boundaries. I remind myself often that there are women older and wiser than I who have faced and survived similar situations, and they are often willing to share their experience and advice.

BOUNDARIES WITH COWORKERS

The boundaries I learned I needed at work did not just include teaching people how I would tolerate being spoken to as their colleague in an operating room. I not only had to set boundaries with disgruntled and sexist surgeons but also with coworkers e-mailing me and texting me at all hours of the night. I had to set boundaries with unpaid work that would land in my inbox as a "we know you can help us with this," while drowning in work I was being paid to do. I had to learn to set boundaries when it came to speaking engagements, helping mentor and sponsor people, and in being the person to always speak up at meetings. (Professional woman tip: do not allow yourself to consistently be the only woman to speak up at meetings. Avoid the trap of those who are less willing to speak up and pressure YOU into being the person who brings up the elephant in the room. You will receive backlash, while they remain in the "safe" zone and are seen as the team player.)

REFRAMING BEING A WOMAN WITH BOUNDARIES

Oftentimes, when we think of the word *boundary,* we think of restrictions. We think of someone or something that is limiting us or constraining others. But I want us to challenge our thinking on boundaries. Boundaries are truly freedom channels. They allow us to safely operate in this world and not become overwhelmed, over functioning, or overcommitted. Boundaries are love paths; they are anything that makes you feel safer. Boundaries protect you and guard your heart. Boundaries are rest for your soul. They are your instruction manual for how you would like people to treat you. They are an explanation of your preferences. They are not rigid, demanding, or fixed; they can be changed, altered, and fluid. You may have one set of boundaries for one person or groups of people and a different set for others. Boundaries are rational, strong, and allow you to be live in peace. Only you know what boundaries you need; another person cannot determine them for you.

BOUNDARIES WITH E-MAIL

You may be reading this book and think, *why does Sasha need boundaries around e-mail?* Maybe you have no problem reading your e-mails during set times. Maybe you aren't like me and struggle when I see a notification in my inbox. I act like an unread e-mail is a ticking time bomb; how fast can I clear it? My computer will explode if I do not respond ASAP! So, this means that I must have fierce boundaries around my e-mail. Otherwise, it becomes a distraction, an obsession, and completely derails my ability to be productive in other areas of my life. If I let it, I will stop looking at people who are speaking to me as I read an e-mail on my phone. E-mail has come between me and my husband on date nights, interrupted times I'm watching my kids play soccer or basketball, and stole joy on my vacation. Why? Because I didn't stick to my boundaries, and I let myself get sucked into the false belief I had to answer them. So, I have strict e-mail boundaries. You, on the other hand, may not need e-mail boundaries. Only you know what boundaries you need. The cool thing is the Brave Boundary Model can be used anywhere, anytime, and applied to any pain point.

REBEL? PASS THE LIME JUICE

When we think of the word *rebel,* we think of someone who pushes the envelope. We think of a rule breaker, someone who pushes past life's regulations and lives outside the lines. Or, if you grew up in my family, you think of my younger sister, Leah Marie. Leah is four years younger than I, and I can say that a significant majority of my childhood was spent getting Leah out of whatever mischief she found herself in, or trying to avoid near death/risk experiences she called "exploring." Since we both survived our childhood, I can tell you that Leah is one of the most fun people I know. I never laugh harder with any other person than I do with her. To know her is to laugh. She brings the fun (and limes; seriously, limes) to any situation. What most of us see as *rules,* Leah sees simply as *suggestions.* She joyfully will find a way to stretch whatever guidelines are in place.

Like the time she decided to bring lime juice directly from her refrigerator through TSA on a trip we were taking. "Why do we need lime juice?" I asked her.

"For margaritas! Duh!" she responded.

When I reminded her we were heading to a nice resort where we could buy a margarita, she reminded me they were not her margaritas, and we were not drinking premixed, fake sugar margs. When I told her the lime juice bottle would not make it through airport security, she shrugged. As I went through precheck, and she waited in the normal line, I rolled my eyes and whispered, "See ya on the other side." Guess who emerged from the Transportation Security Administration line grinning ear to ear, and did the victory "arms up" as I stood there shaking my head? Yes. Leah Marie. This is just one example of how she rolls.

When we think of being a woman with boundaries, we think of being someone who follows the rules and abides by the expectations. But I want you to blow that vision of a woman with boundaries up. Because the truth is, being a woman with boundaries means getting through airport security with lime juice. It means operating against the grain of society and what others expect you to do. Just like everyone in the operating room expected me to shake and sweat when a surgeon thirty years older and more experienced than I started yelling at me, the world does not expect women to bravely set boundaries. But that is an example of what is required of you—not to be a rule follower but a rebel. Being a woman with boundaries means embracing the fact you will have to argue a bit, push against the norm of society, and get uncomfortable. You will have to change the way you currently operate in your home, at work, and with your family and friends. You will have to tap into that courage, that inner strength, and find your brave. Digging fence posts takes muscle; it requires a little sweat equity, and you will burn major calories. Being a woman with boundaries requires courage and fortitude; you will have to go against the grain, set your feet on solid ground, and prepare for some backlash. Being a woman with boundaries means you will have to be a boundary rebel.

As we begin to unpack what it means to be a boundary rebel, I want you to take a deep breath as you steel yourself to embrace it. Close your eyes and whisper to yourself, *I am brave. I am courageous. I can do this.*

You got this, sister. You are becoming a boundary rebel.

Ready?

Boundary Check-In

Take a moment and think of an area of your life that would improve if you had a boundary around it.

1. When you think of setting a boundary, what feelings and thoughts come to your mind? Do you feel stress, anxiety, dread, or fear?

2. Break down that feeling by asking yourself what is it about setting the boundary that brings that feeling? It is setting the boundary in your own mind or is it communicating the boundary?

3. Ask yourself what is the worst-case scenario that would occur if you set the boundary. Go through a mock boundary-setting moment in your mind. If you set the boundary and communicate it, and the worst-case scenario happened, how would you react? Do you know the worst-case scenario that would happen?

4. Reflect on this question: what would be more freeing for you, setting the boundary or avoiding it because of the fear or dread you have? Now imagine the best-case scenario that would occur in response to setting your boundary. How do you feel?

5. Setting boundaries requires us to go against the culture, especially as women. How do you feel when you think of yourself as a boundary rebel? What comes to mind?

CHAPTER 8

BEING A BOUNDARY REBEL

HOW TO EMBRACE DISAPPOINTING NICE PEOPLE

The difference between successful people and really successful people is that really successful people say "no" to almost everything.[xxiv, xxvii]

—Warren Buffett

When the 2020 pandemic hit, it shook our world—no matter where you lived or what your daily job required—our equilibrium was pulled out from underneath us. We were suddenly on unstable and unpredictable ground. We had to flex to care for family members, teach our children virtually at home, and figure out how to remain in the workforce while keeping our families safe. For the majority of us, our responsibilities grew, and our resources were either limited or lessened. We had less domestic help, fewer support systems, and decreased help with in-home care. We became full-time caregivers, teaching assistants, and part-time coaches. We found ourselves doing things we had not done in decades, all while trying to balance the demands of a stressed work force. For those of us living in the United States, on top of the pandemic, we were faced with critical social injustice issues being brought to the surface, an election year dividing us, and fires, floods, and other natural disasters. To say 2020 brought people to a level of unprecedented stress is to speak lightly of an incredibly difficult year.

About six months prior to the pandemic, in the fall of 2019, I began to feel unsettled. There was a sense of restlessness within me, specifically when it came to what I was doing with the company I founded to help professional women, Brave Enough. Increasingly, at three in the morning, I found myself awake and asking, *What is your vision? What is your purpose? Are you living it?*

If you are like me, there are times in life when you deeply question what you are doing, and where you are going. Usually, these times come in my life when I am free from the distractions of life (on vacation somewhere quiet and calm—think beach, margarita in hand), and in the wee hours of the morning when my inner spirit awakens and my mind starts down the rabbit hole of deep contemplation and thought. Why these thoughts never come to me at 3:00 PM when I am well rested, instead of 3:00 AM is one of the questions I am going to ask God when I meet Him someday. Seriously though, *why?*

THE STRENGTH TO DO HARD THINGS

I started to think of what I was doing with my time and energy. At the beginning of each year, I take myself on a retreat of sorts. My retreat involves a day when I write down my goals for the coming year and, more importantly, take inventory of what and where I am spending my time, energy, and money. I ask myself: does my time and money align with my goals? Every year I find that there are projects, people, and appearances I am keeping to please others that don't bring me into line with my purpose and mission. I find it is not hard to set goals for myself for the year; that is the easy part. The more difficult thing is removing things from my life that I am doing simply to please others or feed my ego that do not result in me achieving my purpose.

After taking inventory in January 2020, a hard truth became very clear to me. I was spending one hour a day, on average, in my social media group for women doctors that had grown to nearly thirteen thousand members. I was in year five of running this community, and I had spent years investing in this beautiful group. The community had grown so large, that cultivating it required me to pay outside staff to manage membership and access, and I had to spend more and more time daily maintaining a positive and encouraging culture. I spent on average an hour before work, and an hour after completing my parenting responsibilities in the late evening, responding to direct messages, coaching women who had tagged me in posts and questions in the group, encouraging members who were struggling, reviewing requests, and promoting the women in the group. When I was on call for twenty-four hours or more at the hospital, or my job as a leader required me in the evenings, I would not engage for a day or two. When I would be unavailable for twenty-four to forty-eight hours due to work duties, it soon became apparent I couldn't take a day off. The more I was away from the group, the more things would implode. I made the decision that I must release the group. When

I looked at all of the things I wanted to do—coach smaller groups of women on a deeper level, write this book, connect with my kids nightly without interruption—I knew I could not do these things and continue to run a large community online. I told myself I had six months: six months to do some research, plan the transition, and figure out my exit strategy.

I share this story because it proves that if you're waiting for the perfect time to implement boundaries, you'll be waiting a long time. Something happened in early March 2020; the COVID-19 pandemic hit all health centers full force, and my community online of women physicians felt it, front and center. Social injustice came to the forefront of our daily lives with the murder of George Floyd, and we were in the middle of a tumultuous election year that was causing massive anxiety and stress. While my team would gently ask at our meetings, "What is our plan?" I would shrink and say, "I cannot abandon my group. I have to keep it open for them. These women need me."

The truth is, I didn't want to enforce the boundaries I knew I had to set. I ignored the warning signs that were telling me it was time to transition the group. I avoided the decision knowing I would face enormous backlash and the feeling of letting others down. I did not believe I had the energy or the strength to do the hard things. I was so afraid of the backlash that I ignored what my smart mentors, my closest friends, and people who cared for me were encouraging me to do.

Like other working women in 2020, I was struggling on the home front to help my family and struggling to help the women I was serving in my group. I tried convincing myself I could handle the increasing needs of others and my own well-being, but I found myself failing. Big-time.

FALLING APART TO FALL FORWARD

By September 2020, I was the definition of the hot-mess express. The more I tried to do the right thing online, the more I realized there were no right answers. The pandemic was hard, and people were angry. I was trying to balance being a full-time mom, full-time physician, and full-time leader. My stress was at an all-time high, and I couldn't open my phone without feeling a sense of equal parts dread and fear. What had I missed? What had I not said? What had I not responded to? What had I said? Who was mad at me today? Basically, I was experiencing what every leader of people undergoing trauma, unrest, and fear experiences: a small, albeit loud, mob that was hurling poo at me. I didn't know how to process or handle it except to smile and take it.

My reaction to the backlash was similar to how I think many women react when we face life's hardships. *What is wrong with me? Why can't I handle the criticism and insults and unrest better? Why am I not strong enough? Why am I feeling anxious? I am weak. I am a bad person.*

I got to the point where I could barely get through a day without having massive anxiety. I was hiding my feelings of failure from my husband, who had been encouraging me to transition the group for a year. Instead, I was turning to a nightly glass of wine to forget about all the ways I was letting others down. When we, as women, cannot fix the hurt or pain of others, we tend to blame ourselves. Instead of holding space and recognizing we can't fix all the world's problems, we take on the shame for failing to make all the world's problems disappear.

A SLIVER OF BRAVE

Finally, in late 2020, I found my sliver of brave. I named my company *Brave Enough,* because I am constantly reminded that I need to be just enough brave for the day. I felt *just enough brave* to reach out to a friend who is a psychiatrist and asked her for a recommendation for a therapist. Feeling like a failure for having to seek mental help, I was terrified someone would find out. How would anyone in the group respond when they knew their leader was breaking down inside? Surely, it would make everything worse. The truth is, I thought I was hiding my distress from my family. But I wasn't. My kids were suffering, because I was suffering. My marriage was struggling, because I was falling apart. When you are not well, your relationships suffer. The people you love most suffer with you.

I went to the therapist and told her the truth is that I felt massive shame. I sat in her office and wept for a solid hour. The time felt like only ten minutes as I told her how I was letting so many women down and my family down by not being able to lead better. I explained to her that I felt completely suffocated and paralyzed. I told her I could not see a way out of what I had created, and I didn't know how to transition my work into a more positive effort and group that would allow me to pursue different aims, while protecting my own health. I told her I did not feel authentic, because I was being held hostage by people on the internet who were angry at me for anything I said or didn't say. I had lost trust in myself.

She calmly and sternly spoke to me with equal parts direction and compassion. It was just what I needed. "What you are describing is that you are in a very unhealthy and abusive relationship," she said. "You need boundaries, and you need them ASAP. You cannot be all, or do all, for all people. You have created a complex belief that only you can help solve all the problems women in your community are facing, and you can't."

Her words terrified me. I sat in her office crying. "But there are some amazing women in this group!" I argued. "I simply cannot let them down. I can't let go. Everyone will hate me, and it will be so hard." She smiled at me. I am sure she was thinking, *Oh boy, do I have my work cut out for me.*

I wish I could tell you I wised up and listened to her after one session. But the truth is, I didn't. It took me a few months to see that setting boundaries and dealing with the backlash would be less painful than continuing to stay unwell.

My therapist would calmly point out two main points about boundaries. The first truth is that we have a right to be treated with respect and dignity, regardless of what is happening in the world. The second is that I could not help all women no matter how sad or desperate their situation. I was not well myself, and I needed to focus on putting my own family and health back together. To do that, I needed boundaries.

BOUNDARIES AT YOUR LOWEST POINT: ASK FOR HELP

This experience taught me such an important lesson. Was I willing to adopt boundaries? Was I willing to dig fence posts? The thought of setting boundaries and closing this group after five years 24/7 of blood, sweat, and tears, taking no days off, felt so radical to me, I just couldn't imagine doing it. "You are not the first woman in this situation," my therapist told me. "Reach out to other women; there have to be other women who have done similar things," she encouraged me.

In other words, ask for help. You see, my therapist (who is wonderful, by the way) taught me some valuable lessons. She helped me see that what I was desperately missing were brave boundaries. Sometimes, when you are struggling with how to set boundaries or to even identify the boundaries you need, you need to ask for help. You need to outsource and get ideas from other people who have faced similar situations and set boundaries.

Eventually, I understood I had to follow what I knew was healthy for me and best for my family and my future. I could not move forward in my mission for *Brave Enough* if I was still holding on to something I needed to let go of. How could I be the mom, the leader, the wife I was being called to be if I was spending hours a day in an unhealthy space, pleasing people for fear of being unliked and misunderstood?

BORROWING BOUNDARIES AND STRENGTH FROM OTHERS

I found some important people to help me make the transition. I found women who had done something similar and transitioned communities to smaller ones, who were willing to share the mistakes they made. I found women who were willing to walk next to me as I shared with my group that I was closing it down. My team was so good to me as I faced the boundary backlash. They protected me from a lot of the initial backlash and messages that came in. When you are standing in the pit of life, you learn who your real friends are. The truth is, I would not have found the courage to set the boundaries I needed to set alone. I spent months talking through my fear with my therapist, going over the plan with my team, and listening to the wise words of women who were good enough to offer me their wisdom from similar experiences. Maybe you are staring in the face of a huge mess that you know requires radical boundaries, and you are unable to see your way out or how to start digging one fence post. Do not be afraid to ask for help; you will be amazed at what other women have been through and what wisdom you can glean from them if you ask.

RADICAL BOUNDARIES, RADICAL HEALING

Now, let me tell you this: what I did was no small feat. In fact, I can tell you it was one of the hardest things I have had to do in my life. The backlash was intense, and in the middle of it, it hurt deeply. I left all online groups, decreased my social media presence by 90 percent, and began a process of profound healing that began with radical boundaries. The fallout of my decisions was not easy. I was in a dark place for months, and I felt betrayed by many. But I also learned an incredibly valuable lesson that only comes after choosing yourself over pleasing others.

The more you give yourself away, the more people will take from you. Not everyone who takes from you will give back to you when you need it. It does not mean you shouldn't be you and freely give, but you must choose whom you give to, and, more importantly, your why.

I realized that when I give myself to others now, I ask myself, *Am I giving to this person time and energy expecting nothing in return?* If the answer is yes, then I give it freely. But if not, I don't do it for free. My time is not free. My mental well-being is not free. My wisdom is hard earned. My expertise came at a cost. And thus, it is not for free.

The backlash I faced for setting boundaries on who had access to me and how I spent my time and energy was more radical as the boundaries I had enforced. The fallout from setting these boundaries was debilitating, devastating, and emotionally draining for about eight weeks of my life. I experienced trauma from the backlash sent to me. It was deeply painful. But it was also right, and while I wouldn't wish what I experienced on anyone, I would do it all again in a heartbeat. Why?

Because setting boundaries on who I allowed in and how I allowed them to treat me was the healthiest gift I could give myself. It was what I needed to heal my soul, and it allowed me to start living my life, instead of numbing myself from the pain of it.

DISAPPOINTING NICE PEOPLE

The most difficult thing for me was not the hateful words I received from some. It was not seeing unkind posts in groups from people I thought were my friends. The worst part was letting down women I liked. The most difficult thing to process was disappointing nice people. You see, if you are going to be a boundary rebel, not only are you going to have to do hard things, but you are also going to have to disappoint people you truly care about. You are going to have to say no to people you love and tell people you count as friends that there are times you are simply not available. You are going to have to let people know your preferences and show them how you prefer to be treated. And some of these people, maybe most of these people, are well meaning folks whom you really like.

When we feel like we let someone down or disappointed someone, we feel shame. Shame can be a very powerful emotion that keeps us back from setting boundaries or causes us to doubt the boundaries we set. We may feel guilt. We may not face serious backlash or receive hate mail like I experienced when I closed my Facebook group, but we may start to feel that setting boundaries is wrong.

We, as women, are taught that the measure of our success as a human is the number of people who like us.

At the end of the day, if we feel our ability to set boundaries is limited by people not liking us, we can convince ourselves that setting boundaries is the wrong thing to do.

THE LIKABILITY ADDICTION

I was terrified to let people down. Not only was I dreading the backlash, I was also terrified thinking about all the people who would not like me anymore. I had become addicted to likeability, and in the process, lost my own mental peace. Here is the dangerous thing about living a life with no boundaries: the more you please others, the more it fills your ego. You become used to the daily hit of being liked, receiving praise, being the person who is always there for others and never disappoints anyone. It becomes an addiction. It's similar to the endorphins you get when you take an opiate—the praise and likes you receive from pleasing others gives you a high. It makes you feel special for a moment. You feel good to be liked and needed. You begin down a dangerous path your ego leads you on: *only I can help this person, or answer this call, or do this work.* While you may feel completely empty, at the same time the likes and attention you receive from others fills that emptiness, and you become accustomed to living your life for praise and the affection of others.

But eventually, you crash. You burn out. Ultimately, you won't be able to say yes enough. Your ability to deliver everything to everyone will fall short. You are human after all. And as the emptiness and fatigue becomes a widening canyon between who you are and who you desperately want to be, suddenly there is no amount of likes or favor in the eyes of others that can rescue you and bridge the gap. You find yourself falling off the cliff, wondering how your attempt to do everything for others, to be the best for others, to show up for others and do your part, has allowed you to fall so short.

Only you can operationalize your boundaries.

Most of us have a hard time equating pleasing others with boosting our ego. It is easier to place the blame on why we can't set boundaries on others. But we must remember what we discussed prior: Only you can set boundaries for yourself, and only you can communicate your boundaries to others. How others respond to your boundaries is outside your control. As we embrace being a boundary rebel, we have to take ownership of the reality that our own ego and desire to be liked is inhibiting us from setting boundaries. Boundary rebels are aware of their egos. They recognize the likeability trap lurking in the shadows. Boundary rebels bravely take on boundaries and are willing to face boundary backlash. They choose the freedom from people-pleasing over the ego boosts that come with pleasing others. They choose peace and well-being over popularity and praise.

DEALING WITH BOUNDARY BACKLASH

When we begin to set boundaries, we change. We alter the way we communicate and express our needs and wishes with others. When we begin to communicate our preferences and our abilities openly with others in any area of our lives, it is only natural that we will experience backlash. Our world is not used to women directly and unapologetically expressing their wants and desires. It is a predictable outcome of women setting boundaries, and it is to be expected when we begin to live our priorities.

All of us have different personalities that I believe are fueled by four different pillars: our core fear, our motivation, our core longing, and our weakness. We deal with boundary backlash in different ways, as we are completely different people. It is important to note that there is not one perfect or right way to deal with backlash. I am going to summarize different methods for dealing with backlash, and they all have value. The most important lessons to gain in this chapter are that backlash will happen, and how you deal with it is entirely up to you. I am going to summarize the different techniques you can utilize to deal with boundary backlash. These skills are extremely effective and powerful and should be part of every woman's toolkit. Think of yourself as walking into a closet full of different weapons, preparing to do battle. Which weapons will you choose?

When I think of the different ways you can face the battles ahead, I think of all the different women I have encountered in my life who have shared their stories with me of when they've finally had enough and decided to pick up the battle ax. No two stories are the same, but the underlying theme is similar. Most women I know, who have decided to step into their power and set radical boundaries, can name a defining moment of undoing. It may have been an e-mail where they were voluntold to take on a new unpaid task not in their job description. It may have been a text message from work on their vacation. It may have been a microaggression clothed in a comment from a colleague meant to take a jab at their confidence. It may have been a realization they aren't being paid equitably. It may have been walking into the laundry room and seeing ten piles of laundry others expect them to do. There are many ways women may reach their breaking point, when they decide taking the backlash from setting boundaries is far less detrimental to their mental health and well-being than being taken advantage of one more time.

Have you ever experienced that moment when you think to yourself, *If one more person asks me for something, I am going to run away.* Have you ever had a moment when you were pushed to take on another task, and you thought to yourself, *I can't do this, I am done.* Have you ever experienced a moment when you start to read another e-mail asking you for something and suddenly you want to drop everything you are carrying and *scream at the top of your lungs for as long as you can?*

BOUNDARY BACKLASH TOOLKIT

You may get to the point of needing radical boundaries in differing routes, but when you have arrived, you know it's time. And how you deal with the backlash is likely as different as the path that brought you to realize you need boundaries in the first place. Here are some tools you can use to deal with the backlash:

1. **Saying "Thank you."** Yep. Two words. These two words are incredibly disarming and a powerful weapon to use on anyone who sends you raging backlash out of anger for your boundaries. For example, simply writing *Thank you for your feedback* can be used to respond to an e-mail where someone has laid into you for setting boundaries that they aren't on board with. Saying *Thank you* also works when someone confronts you in the moment and tries to make you say *yes* instead of the *no* you just stated. It actually works even when someone is

projecting their anger or frustration onto you, and you have had enough. A firm thank you causes the person who is giving you backlash to stop. It stuns them. They aren't sure how to take a thank you. You are not conceding your position. You are holding firm to the boundary you set. But you are saying, thank you, but enough. I appreciate the feedback, and now I am moving on to more productive things. (Note: I suggest saying *thank you* with a smile but leaving your hands down, if at all possible. This is just a suggestion from someone who finds it hard not to talk with her hands and has found that leaving them at my sides is less threatening when I smile and say, *thank you* and move on.)

2. **Breathing and releasing.** Take one minute and breathe. Then release the backlash. The truth is, you do not need to respond, verbally or in written form, to every form of backlash or criticism you receive for setting boundaries. Sometimes it is just best to leave it where it is and hit delete. Depending on our personality traits, our life's circumstances, and the person(s) giving us the backlash, the appropriate response may be breathing and releasing. Taking a moment to process the backlash, catching your breath and moving on is a response. Only you know what is right one for you. Do not allow someone else to pick out your tools for battle. You know what feels best in your hand.

3. **Engage in a brief but firm manner.** Sometimes the right thing is to confront the backlash head on. Perhaps the person won't take *no* for an answer or begins to demonstrate retaliatory behavior for you setting boundaries. Remember, we all have

different boundaries, and your boundaries may appear completely bizarre to another person. I've learned in life that when people do not understand something, often their first reaction is to stomp on it like they would a bug they see crawling across the floor. It is never fun to be stomped on, and sometimes we have to repeat the boundary, firmly, and then move on. It does not serve you, or the other person, to engage with someone who is angry, retaliatory, or frustrated. Being firm and moving on quickly gives two things every person needs at some point in their life: grace and space.

4. **Give specific and unemotional instruction.** I have learned that the following statements used verbally or in written form can be helpful to me when I am dealing with different forms of backlash.

- Thank you. I prefer to discuss this in person. Feel free to set up a time to chat.
- Thank you for your feedback. I am moving on.
- I prefer to be talked to respectfully.
- I appreciate your feedback. My answer is unchanged.
- I am unable to do what you are asking, as it does not fit in my year's goals.
- I can see/sense you are frustrated. I will give you space.
- Thank you for allowing me to hear your feelings/thoughts.

These are a just a few statements I have used. And when I say this is how I respond, I mean, this is literally all I say/write before walking away or hitting send. The briefer you keep your response to backlash, the quicker it dissipates. You simply cannot expect everyone to give you a round of applause when you set a boundary, and you must be prepared to get some backlash. But you do not need to respond to each piece with a dissertation. Again, breathing and releasing *is* a response and may be the best one in certain circumstances.

The best news is, like any hard situation, if you remain calm and seated in your foundation, each day will get a little bit better. You are not responsible for people's reactions to your boundary setting. Being a boundary rebel will cause backlash. Expect it. Prepare for it. And don't forget to breathe.

Boundary Check-In

By now you have hopefully identified an area of your life where you recognize you need boundaries. Take a moment to walk yourself through what it would look like to set the boundary and address any potential backlash that may come as a result.

1. Imagine you have shared your boundary with those who need to hear it.

2. The response to this is that the person(s) is first surprised, then starts to ask you why you are doing this. Imagine they become angry and start to speak in an aggressive manner, and you start feeling small and ashamed for setting the boundary.

3. Based on the toolkit listed above, what is your best response to their anger? Walk yourself through which of the tools makes the most sense to you and feels the most comfortable to you.

4. What outcomes in your life would change after you were able to live within these boundaries? Write down these outcomes. How would you feel knowing you have set this boundary? Write down the feeling(s).

CHAPTER 9

HOW MANY TIMES DO I HAVE TO TELL YOU? (A LOT)

BOUNDARY MANAGEMENT: CLARIFYING YOUR BOUNDARIES EVERY DAY

Boundaries keep more than the bad out of our lives.
They also keep the good in.

—Sandy Schoville (the best mother on earth)

At this point in my life, utilizing a "vacation" day from my paid time-off bank means something much different than it did when I was starting out as an early career physician. In the first decade of my career in medicine, every day was a battle of survival, trying to climb the rungs of academia, while balancing four kids at home, ensuring they all made it to adulthood unscathed without spending time in juvie. For a solid decade, I'd save my paid time off from the hospital for those few weeks a year where Lance and I would pack up swim diapers, approximately 765 bottles of sunscreen, oversized rash guards, and an ungodly number of fruit snacks for the plane trip, while attempting to get through TSA with eighteen suitcases, a double stroller, and booster seats before someone threw a tantrum or spilled baby oat puffs (what the heck are those, anyway?). All the while we were praying the enormous preparation to head to some destination to "relax" wouldn't be in vain when one of your tiny people leans over to you on the airplane and says, "Mom, I think I'm going to puke."

If you have ever been at the beach for a week with small children, you are probably laughing out loud at the thought of this being an actual escape where you recharge and find your internal peace. When you are a mother of four, there is no resting in a hammock sipping a concoction of fresh pineapple and rum. There is sand however, and it is everywhere. Tiny granules of sand become a reminder that you are not in fact going to make it through one chapter of the beach read you bought off Amazon at 3:00 AM while packing, and there is no butler service. There is sand in crevices of small bodies mixed with PABA-free sunblock belonging to people telling you their brother just dropped their sandwich in the tide pool.

Along with the sand, there are tears when you have to pull them out of the water to reapply SPF 70 so they don't end up looking like midwestern children at the beach on day two who are burnt to a crisp. There is shortness of breath as you spend the first fifty-five minutes at the beach wrestling them to lather sunscreen so as to avoid inhalation of the spray, which you now believe may cause cancer because some well-meaning colleague sent you the latest medical study related to sunscreen to help prepare you for your trip. There is confusion, as to why you decided to spend your entire hard-earned bonus on what feels like more work than your normal week parenting on the face of Hades. But instead of thinking too deeply on these facts, you are quickly interrupted by someone who is hungry. Soon, you're off to the races armed with a forty-five dollar bottle of cancer-free sunscreen you also found on Amazon. Bless.

There is also massive fear of what may be lurking in the shallow water. You pictured you'd be sipping something sparkly out of a wine shaped Yeti, watching your offspring gleefully frolic on the beach in matching swimsuits. Instead, you spend the entire time on the beach, death scanning. Yes, death. *Was that a fin? Where is the body board they were just playing with? Where is the third child? How deep is she in the water?* Basically, you're scanning for potential fatalities. *Is that another fin?* By the time you've done the body count on the sand, it's time to lather your people again.

At the end of the day, you look at your husband as you collapse on the bed in the rental house and say, "Wow, this was fun." Yes. This is your vacation. This is your rest. As you walk into work that Monday, you can still feel sand in your scalp. Completely wiped out, you yawn when you walk into the hospital at an ungodly hour, and as you pass your partner at the coffee cart, he yells across the atrium, "Welcome BACK! How was your vacation?"

NO MORE SAND: VACATION BOUNDARIES

After getting four children through elementary school, I have wised up. I have completely changed how I use my vacation days. My time is the most valuable asset I have, besides my children and my health. My time off is mine. Period. I carry my vacation days close to my heart like I'm protecting a precious jewel. And while I still spend about half of my vacation days doing things like traveling to out-of-town soccer events, heading to the beach with my family, and the occasional amusement park, I have developed radical boundaries around 50 percent of my paid time off. I am talking about this here, because the most difficult boundaries we often have to set are with the people we love the most. Having boundaries around my vacation days means I have had difficult and honest conversations with my best friend—my husband—and my family. And let me tell you, when you set boundaries, you will find you have to reinforce them and do what I call boundary management, over and over.

You cannot expect to explain or set a boundary once and everyone will remember it. They won't.

When it comes to my time off, I have decided that I am in charge of my time off, and therefore it is up to me on how I use these days. I realized after years of exhaustion that for me, personally, if I use 100 percent of my paid time off to travel and for family excursions, which may or may not include days of rest, I burn out and become emotionally and physically exhausted. So, about six years ago, I did a brave thing; I started using half of my vacation days for me. For my well-being. For my reset. For my sanity.

The most difficult boundaries we have to set are with the people we love the most.

I remember the first time I took a random day off in the middle of the week to recover from a brutal string of work travel, soccer and sports-packed weekends, crazy cardiac calls, and overwhelming work demands. I found myself driving home from work in tears. The thought of going to work the next day made me feel hopeless.

I wasn't sure how I was going to face all the parenting duties I had to do that night, and show up for my people until I could crash into bed. The thought of doing the same thing the next day and fully showing up for my patients was paralyzing. I found myself sitting in my garage tearful, anxious, and lacking the energy to get out of the car and go inside to face my second shift of work.

As I sat in my car, I knew I needed to pull back. I needed desperately to unplug for a day and rest. I needed to be away from people, turn off my phone, and not be responsible for what I call "heartbeats." I didn't even have the energy to pet my dog, Jack, whom I could see waiting at the door for me. The thought of giving Jack any attention was too much for me. I needed a day off, stat.

I called the person who set the operating room schedule for the next day and asked if there was room in the schedule for me to take a day off and use a vacation day. "Is everything okay?" my partner asked. "Yes, of course. Everything is fine," I lied.

Everything was not fine. I was not fine. And I knew it. But at this point, I was still early in figuring out these things called boundaries and how to self-regulate my own well-being and diminish the overwhelm. I was starting to dig out of the hole I had created for myself, and while I was on my way to living an empowered life with healthy time management that included radical boundaries, I was just dipping my toe into running my own life. Truly.

So, I took the next day off. As my husband was getting ready for work the next day at 5:30 AM, he asked if I was going to get in the shower. "No. I am not going to work today," I said quietly. He stared at me. He asked why. I explained I had taken a day of vacation. When I told him this, it was like he couldn't process it. "Vacation? Are you going somewhere? Are you okay? Is everything okay?" he asked, in a worried voice.

I am not lying when I tell you I found myself standing in my bathroom, summoning up immense courage of which I had little. On top of complete exhaustion, I felt a deep sense of shame. Yes. Shame. For taking a random vacation day. For "using up" my precious few paid time-off days to simply rest. I suddenly felt like I was the most selfish woman on the planet, and that I should be able to go to work and do all the things mothers do and not be tired. It was as if I was admitting defeat to my husband, that my failure as a physician and a mom had led me to be selfish, use a vacation day, and basically engage in inappropriate behavior for a mom and a woman with a family. In that moment, I wanted to take it all back and tell my husband I would just go to work. There is no other word to describe what I felt in that moment other than shame.

BOUNDARIES REQUIRE VULNERABILITY

When you lack boundaries, it is often the people in your life who you think it will be easiest to explain your need for boundaries to who are most difficult. We find it most arduous to explain and enforce boundaries to people who deeply love us. Why? Because boundaries require vulnerability. They require us to take a sledgehammer to the walls we have built around our own needs, our own wants, and our well-being. Essentially, we are saying to those closest to us, *I need to be well today. I am choosing me, and thus I need to withdraw from you, and from everyone else who depends on me, and refuel. I need to fill my empty cup, and that is only filled by me being alone, in solitude.*

Let me tell you, that takes courage. Why? Because we are most afraid of hurting those we love. We are most afraid of sending a message of "I am not available" to those we care for the most, those we are most responsible for in life: our kids, our spouses, our supervisors, our parents, our best friends, our closest colleagues.

But what we find is that the opposite is the truth. Those who love and respect us will likely be most understanding of our need to be well. They have most to gain from us setting radical boundaries around our time and well-being. And while the conversation, in the moment, will feel sticky and messy and may invoke feelings of shame, I promise you that when you share your boundaries and your need to protect your mental health with those who care about you, the result is deep love and respect. Because you are saying to them, *You can share your boundaries now with me, too.*

For the last seven years, I have changed my mindset of what a "vacation day" means to me. Plenty of them are used for special trips with my family, but an equal number are used for random Wednesdays when I need to pull back. I wake up and ride my bike. I go to breakfast by myself. I write. I clean out a closet I've been waiting to do for months. Sometimes I have lunch with a friend. Sometimes I lay outside on my deck in a chair and shed tears for some grief I am going through. Nearly always, I spend time in prayer. And every time, I feel better. I feel closer to the real me, and I feel hope. The only way I know how to reset myself is to withdraw into solitude.

I wish I could tell you that when I say "I am off tomorrow" that everyone in my family says, "Have a great day, Mom!" but that does not happen; even after years of doing this. Do you hear me? *I have been a boundary rebel for over seven years now, and my people are still convinced they can take me on.* What this means is that I have to routinely set boundaries and share them with my husband, my kids, and my family that say: *I am not available for you *insert*, I am choosing me.* Many times, my husband will say, "Oh, good! You're

off tomorrow? I need you to pick up *insert child* at school." Or,
"Oh, perfect! Your car needs an oil change. Can you drop it off?"
The truth is, I could do all of these things on the random days I
select to recharge. I could pick up kids from the school or shuffle
them to soccer. I could do oil changes or go to the dry cleaner. *But
it is not what I promised myself I would do, and unless it is on my rest
plan, I need to stick to my boundaries.* I promised myself I would set
the boundary of my day and do things I had planned for my own
mental health. It has taken me years, and I mean years, to reinforce
boundaries with my husband. But more importantly, it has taken me
an equal amount of time to honor my own boundaries with myself.

HONORING BOUNDARIES WITH YOURSELF

What tends to happen on these precious Sasha-wellness recharge
days is that I wake up at 5:30 a.m. and resist the urge to get up and
start cleaning the house. I walk into the kitchen to make myself
coffee and have to stop myself from making a monster breakfast for
my crew out of guilt. Then, I start to see stacks of mail I could go
through, junk I could purge in the pantry, and notifications on my
e-mail inbox that have trickled in overnight. *You should work for an
hour and THEN rest,* my internal workaholic-self starts whispering.
I have to self-coach to stick with my plan. My internal dialogue normally goes something like this.

> *I am a boundary rebel, so I use boundaries to manage
> my time.*
>
> *I will honor myself today by honoring my boundaries.*
>
> *I want my kids to have healthy boundaries, so I will
> model healthy boundaries.*

I want to have energy to be the woman I want to be, so I am sticking to my boundaries today.

I want to be a woman of focus; boundaries protect my focus.

My kids and my husband deserve the best me. I will rest to bring her back.

My patients deserve the best Dr. Shillcutt there is; I am going to stick to my rest plan today.

I don't know about you, but I strive to be a woman of her word. I want to be the kind of woman who shows up when she says she is going to. I desire to be a woman who others can trust. I want to be a woman who others can count on. I want to be a woman who gets the job done. I want to be a woman who, when she says, *I got this,* means it.

You Cannot Be That Woman Unless You Have Radical Boundaries.

Boundaries protect your energy. Boundaries give you immense focus. Boundaries protect your energy, and thus boundaries protect your word. When you are a woman with boundaries, you are a woman other women respect. When you share your boundaries with others, you will be respected, even if you initially receive backlash. Others will respect you for having the courage to express and share your preferences, protect your focus, and demonstrate your energy saving techniques. When you display to others that you are not afraid of others' expectations or reactions to your boundaries, you level up.

KEEPING THE GOOD IN

And most importantly is this: Boundaries do not just keep what is going off the rails in our life out of your headspace; they keep the good *in*. Boundaries help you have time to achieve joy in your life; they make space for things like relationships, nature walks, vacation planning, and parties. Boundaries allow your brain to have ideas and creativity, not just to-do lists. Boundaries allow you to dream, laugh, and make memories. Once you accept radical boundaries in your life, you have more joy. Instead of focusing on all the things you have to do, you say *no* to all the things that don't fit your priorities. You have radical clarity of what your priorities are, and you start to live them. You schedule that dinner date. You allow yourself to sit in the sun and read a book for an hour. You say yes to your son who asks you to go on a bike ride. You have space, you have energy, and you have well, you.

If you are questioning that being a boundary rebel will bring you joy, think of the women and men in your life you respect; not those you necessarily *like,* but those whom you *respect.* Most of the people we respect are people who have fierce and transparent boundaries, even if those boundaries are not ones we ourselves would choose to adopt. We may respect them because they are able to maintain a life with their priorities constantly in view. They do not lose sight of what is important to them, and pleasing others is not on that list. They maintain a sense of integrity, ethics, and transparency that we greatly respect. How they control their time, who they allow into their circle, what they spend their resources on may be completely opposite of how we would do it, but we respect them because they are principled people. They are selective on where they place their energy, and people with boundaries remain well. They maintain their well-being independent of what is going on around them. In the midst of trials and challenges, they are able to keep their focus on what they know to be valuable and important in life. People with boundaries are resilient; they are strong; and mostly, they have joy. They are not hindered by what other people expect them to do. They keep their eyes on what they know is their mission and priorities. Boundaries allow them to do that.

I want to be a strong person, radically vulnerable enough to share my boundaries, and strong enough to stick with them.

Don't be confused by what I am saying here: there is nothing wrong with people being pleased with our actions, or with doing something that make others proud of us or happy with us. But when we begin to rely solely on the accolades of others, or we feel powerless to say *no,* we lack our own compass. We may have a list of priorities, but they may only live in our head, like a "wish list" we think we can only enforce once our life is stress free. We think to ourselves, *When I get that promotion, then I will say no more to late calls in the evening and on the weekend.* Or, *When I have X amount of money in the bank, I will be able to focus less on my job and more on my well-being.* Or, *Once my kids are grown, I will finally make time for myself and use a vacation day just for me.* We have this idea that once our life hits some level of utopia, we will be brave enough to set boundaries. When we have time and energy, we will suddenly find the courage to tell others of our boundaries.

The truth is, there is never a perfect time to set boundaries.

The best time to set boundaries is now. Your mental health, your physical health, your energy, and your focus are all dependent on your ability to set boundaries. The promise you keep to yourself, and the agreements you keep to others is the strongest predictor of your boundaries. If you are struggling to show up for others in a healthy manner, and you are challenged every day to show up for yourself, this book is perfect: you need boundaries. And the time is now.

BOUNDARIES AND YOUR PERSONALITY TYPE

If you accept boundaries as part of your daily life, then they become easier to implement. A common false belief is that your ability to set boundaries is inherently dependent on your personality, and some people just can't set boundaries. The truth is that boundaries are no different than other elements of our natural social tendencies. I know some incredibly introverted people who are fantastic public speakers. Their ability to teach and reach people is phenomenal, and they are able to overcome stage fright and imposter syndrome to speak to hundreds of others. This doesn't mean that after they attend a large gathering they don't need to withdraw and refill their cup of solitude; they do. They can be incredibly engaging and social, but it requires major energy, unlike me, an extrovert who can walk into a room full of people and feel like I just took a hit of adrenalin.

Just like introverts have to burn some fuel to walk into a room and engage with the masses, some people have to burn more calories to set boundaries than other people. That does not mean you cannot do it or you won't be successful in setting boundaries. Don't use your personality traits or social comfort level as an excuse to not set boundaries. Boundaries are for everyone, regardless of your internal talents, unique personality, and your to-do list. B o u n d - aries are hard for almost every human on the planet, but they are more unexpected and challenging for women. As stated previously, boundaries are counterculture for women. We do not expect women to freely express their boundaries to others, so when they do, others (including ourselves!) may become uncomfortable. We, as women, have to explain our boundaries to others on the regular. That may not be fair, but it is our reality. Boundary rebels don't back away from hard things. Boundary rebels do hard things every day. They eat the expectations of others for lunch and ask for some hot sauce to spice it up. Cholula, anyone?

BOUNDARIES ARE UNIQUE

As we start the process of explaining our boundaries to others, we have to realize that our boundaries are extremely personal. We can't expect other people to know our boundaries or to even understand them. My husband, for example, would never take a day of vacation in solitude by himself. And he is an introvert. He wouldn't think of taking a vacation day for wellness. If he has a day off, he wants to spend it watching soccer or hanging with the kids at the pool. It has taken me a while to explain to him that generally, on my wellness days, I do not want to be around anyone, even people I love. We differ this way, and it is a good example of how it really has to do with what refuels us individually. Before you throw the book across the room and think she is just a stronger person than I am, hold on while I explain this further.

My husband, in many ways, has better boundaries than I ever will. He routinely will state on weekends, *I am going downstairs to watch soccer*. Or, *Sasha, the Chiefs are on Monday Night Football.* Let me translate what this actually means.

Our house can be a next level disaster. Messes everywhere. The grass outside looks like the Unabomber may have lived in our garage. He has zero clean clothes. And he will literally look at me and say, *I am going to the basement to watch sports.* But that is not what he is really saying. What he is expressing to everyone in the household is this: *I am going downstairs. Do not bother me. Do not ask me to do anything. I am tired, and I am going to watch my teams play. I am not going to answer my phone. I am not driving kids anywhere. I am unwinding. Please leave me alone.*

My husband has the ability in the craziest of moments to set radical boundaries. He is the master of everyday boundaries. And honestly, while at times I want to throat punch him for his ability to ignore the fact every surface in our house is sticky, I love this about him. He can have a hundred things to do, the house could be falling apart, and he will look at me and say, *I am going to work out.* And he does. He turns it all off. He steps over dirty clothes and ignores piles of mail and goes and finds bliss for an hour in the gym. Sometimes it still catches me off guard, because it is not easy for me to do what he does and tell everyone he is off the clock for the next hour or so without any backlash or guilt. He sets more routine boundaries than I do, and I respect this about my husband greatly. His boundaries are very transparent; they are very clear to those he does life with. When his phone rings, and he is focused on something, he does not answer it. He ignores nonessential texts for days. And you know what? No one hates my husband for this. No one complains to me about his boundaries. They respect him. He will tell our employees who ask him for something on Thursday, "I will have time for that on Tuesday." Without guilt, without remorse.

My husband doesn't feel like he's being an absent father when he escapes to the basement for four hours to watch soccer. No one makes him feel guilty or judges him for ignoring dishes and laundry and homework. He doesn't beat himself up for setting boundaries around his own mental health and well-being. Why? Our culture respects men who set boundaries. Our society does not question it.

PEOPLE WITH BOUNDARIES EMPOWER PEOPLE WITH BOUNDARIES

Because I have watched my husband set boundaries, I have felt empowered to set my own. He does not always recognize that is what I am doing, but once I decline his asks and put my needs into this context he understands. And he doesn't judge me, he applauds me. *No Babe, I cannot take the car to get an oil change today, I have plans for myself,* I have learned to say to him, guilt free. It has taken me a while, but just as I respect his need to decompress at times and watch the Premier League uninterrupted, he respects my ability to say no and leave the house and spend time with myself.

Here are some statements I have found to be helpful when explaining my boundaries to others.

- I am needing time by myself to sort out some things. So tomorrow, I am unavailable from 8:00 to 12:00. Do we need to ask someone to help with the kids?

- I am not myself. I took the day off tomorrow so I can feel more like me and recharge.

- I am run down. Tomorrow is a rest day for me. Can you think of anything we need to cover?

- Mom is having a wellness day to recharge tomorrow. Thanks for helping Dad so I can rest.

These may sound cheesy to you, and certainly you can explain your boundaries how you want. But notice what I didn't do here: I didn't apologize. I didn't lie or make excuses either. I don't want my family to think they can't express themselves when they are exhausted and burned out. Since I have started doing this, I've noticed my teens will say, "I am really tired, I am going to skip the game with all of you tonight and stay home and rest." And you know what? I support it! I want my kids to feel courageous enough to express when they are emotionally and physically depleted and need time alone in their rooms. I want my kids to feel strong enough to regulate their well-being and tell others they need a break. I want healthy kids, and I hope that I am demonstrating what setting boundaries looks like. No apologies, no excuses, just the truth: *this is what is best for my health and wellness, so I am choosing it.*

Boundary Check-In

One way to test your comfort level with expressing boundaries to others is to hypothetically think of what would happen if you took a day off for yourself.

- First, think of what a day of "you" time would look like. What would you do? What would you not do?

- Second, think of telling the people closest to you—your work colleagues, your family, your partner, best friend, your kids—that you are unavailable for a day as you focus on you. What feelings and thoughts surface? Thoughts of guilt? Thoughts of your never-ending to-do list? Thoughts of being wasteful with your precious time? Would you feel guilt? Shame? Fear? Excitement?

- Think of your best friend; this person calls you and tells you they are burned out, and they desperately need a day off, alone, to rest. What would you think of your best friend as she tells you this? Would you think of her as selfish? Would you encourage her to be well and take a day? Would you offer this same rest to yourself? Why or why not?

CHAPTER 10

JOINING THE BOUNDARY REVOLUTION: THE NEW (FIERCE) YOU

THRIVING WITHIN THE FENCE, MOVING FORWARD WITH BOUNDARIES

You've always had the power, my dear,
you just had to learn it yourself.

—Glinda the Good Witch

A few years ago, I began doing a literature review on time management in preparation for speaking at the Harvard Women's Leadership Course, *Career Advancement and Leadership Skills for Women in Healthcare,* organized by my colleague and friend Dr. Julie Silver each fall in Boston. As I was studying articles as evidence for my teaching, it struck me that one theme seemed to be prevalent in research studies about leaders, students, and employees who have stellar abilities to manage their time: they believe they control it. Successful people have self-agency. According to this meta-analysis, which reviewed hundreds of studies on people who manage their time well, one of strongest predictors of having strong time-management skills is an individual having an "internal loci of control."[xxix] In other words, people who are able to balance many things and have good time management skills share an inherent belief: they are in control of their calendars, their schedules, and, therefore, their time. They are able to manage their time well because they believe they are in charge of it.

I chuckled to myself as I read this report, because I realized this is what I had been teaching women in my courses as a solid foundation for years—you must believe you are in charge of YOU. You must believe you are your own CEO. If you do not believe this, you essentially are handing over control of your life to your boss, your kids, your spouse, your work colleagues, or whatever person needs you. You are essentially moving through each day by waking up and saying, *Who needs me today? Who is going to control me today? Who is the boss of me, today?*

YOU ARE LEADING YOU

Here is the thing: someone will always be there to be the boss of you. In fact, when you leave your house, imagine a line of cars waiting outside for you. Each of them is there to drive you to a different location, for you to work for them. They are there waiting for you to get in and hand over all control. Perhaps one car is your boss. In one car is your family. In another, your work colleagues, or that organization that needs you to volunteer. You stand in the driveway conflicted. *Which car should I get into today?*

What I hope this book has taught you is that living well is living empowered. And that comes with the belief that the minute you set your feet on the ground in the morning, *you are leading you.* You cannot expect the cars to not be there, especially if you have been living your life with no boundaries. Do not get angry at all the cars lined up ready to take you to places that need you to fulfill their needs. You have essentially taught them this is okay to do.

Today, when you leave for work, wave to all those people. Smile as you walk to your own car and get in. Because, sister, you are going a different direction today. You are a boundary rebel, and boundary rebels drive their own cars. They turn up the radio and sing on the way to work. They set the temperature where they like it. And they wink at their copilot who is sitting next to them, encouraging them, clapping for them, and speaking truth to them. As a woman of faith, my copilot is Christ. He's got my iPhone open to maps as He says, "Where we going today, Sash?" We all need a copilot—that person who believes in us and helps us have the confidence we need to embrace being a boundary rebel. Maybe yours is a friend, a parent, your spouse, a work colleague, or even your future self.

The amazing thing about being a boundary rebel is that you naturally start to develop radically awesome time-management skills as you believe you are in charge of your own time. When you start to dig holes to hold your fence posts, you begin to slowly take back your time and protect it. Time management is the natural outcome of setting boundaries around your well-being and how you spend your time. You begin to be focused on your priorities because they are in your view as you say *yes* to this and *no* to that.

WHAT BOUNDARY REBELS BELIEVE

There are some key truths that boundary rebels subscribe to. They keep them in the forefront of their mind in life's busiest seasons. They remember them over and over when they feel the overwhelm creeping up. Instead of beating themselves for backsliding and finding themselves overcommitted again, they stop, pull out these truths, straighten their boundary rebel sashes, and adjust their crowns. They get back to being boundary rebels with grit for the work ahead and grace for themselves and others.

One Sunday, I was leaving church and received a desperate message from an amazing leader I know. This leader is not one to bother work colleagues on the weekend unless it is important. When I saw her name on my phone, I instantly stopped to read her message.

She described that she had been called by a work colleague to fix a problem that our work colleague deemed urgent. Not only was she called at home on a Sunday, she had taken the next week off and set an out-of-office message. A colleague was calling with an administrative problem, not a direct patient care problem. In anesthesiology, we have a team of anesthesiologists "in house" (aka, in the hospital) twenty-four hours a day, seven days a week, ready to take care of patients. Thus, the issue, while important, was in no way an emergency or related to urgent patient care. As a leader, she felt compelled to help this work colleague out, even though there were other work colleagues who were on call and being paid to cover this issue on the weekend. She stopped what she was doing and helped the person, which required several text messages, logging on to her computer, calling a few different doctors, reorganizing schedules, and several other administrative tasks. By the time she was done, she had spent over an hour working on the solution to the problem. But surprisingly, that was not why she was reaching out to me.

My colleague, who is a great leader and excellent at her job, was reaching out because she was upset and hurt. She was hurt because that, while she fixed the problem, one of our colleagues was upset with her solution. The colleague called her and yelled at her on the phone. She remained calm but felt completely defeated. Not only had she done work on a Sunday off to help the team, she was chastised for her solution and had to deal with the anger projected at her. She was upset and wanting a listening ear.

I understood her thinking, and I also felt for her as I have been in her exact situation many times. I would venture to say what my colleague experienced has likely been experienced by every working woman on the planet. You go above and beyond your job description, fixing a problem on your non-paid time, and somehow it is not enough. Or worse, you are chastised for how you fixed the problem, and you receive backlash despite your best attempts to help others. Sound familiar?

DAILY SETTING BOUNDARIES

What I told this leader was: "Turn off your phone. Remove your e-mail application, now, from your phone. You can reload it in a week when you are back at work. Do not answer any more phone calls from anyone from the hospital for the next nine days. There are no administrative emergencies that cannot be handled by the leadership team at work. You are not required to work twenty-four hours a day, seven days a week, and you do not owe anyone at your company all your time when you are on scheduled leave."

I also shared with her that she needed to honor the woman she is by honoring her boundaries. So, when the phone rings, let it go to voicemail. As a leader, it is even more vital for you to not only have work-life boundaries, but that you model them for those you work with.

ANY WOMAN CAN BE A BOUNDARY REBEL

If you read my advice to her and inside are screaming, "No way! She is a leader! She is paid to be available! She should be there for people and help!" your ego is likely being triggered. Are you mad yet? I know, I know. You may be asking, "Is she calling me egotistical?" No way! This is how to be a servant leader! I am not egotistical, *I am serving.* Sorry Charlie, but that is your ego talking. Our egos love to judge others, especially ourselves. Our egos are needy children who are constantly fed by the drug of being needed. Our ego likes to say things like, "Only I can fix this problem." My ego's favorite is, "I can fix this problem faster than anyone else, so I will cross my own boundary and help this person." A corollary to this one is, "Everyone will praise me for helping, and I don't want to disappoint anyone. I want to be liked and loved, so I must help." Breaking your own boundaries to help others to be liked is not being a servant, it is being *prideful.* Our egos love to label it as serving others, but believe me when I say your ego will also quickly change the tune from, "I am helping others" to "Ugh! I am so sick of helping others; no one helps me!" when you become overstretched and burned out from the need to please.

The best thing you can do as a working woman who desires to be an effective and respected leader is to be a boundary rebel! Honor the woman you are by honoring your boundaries. To be a boundary rebel is to go against the grain of society's expectations of women to please others at all costs.

When you honor yourself by honoring your own boundaries, you empower women watching you to do the same.

Dr. Cheryl Peters is a pediatric anesthesiologist and intensivist who I have had the privilege to know through my classes and community. "It wasn't that long ago I didn't even know what a boundary was. I said yes to every opportunity in order to advance in my career. I was a people pleaser and had porous boundaries. My strong work ethic resulted in a deep sense of responsibility to others. I didn't recognize it at the time, but my lack of boundaries was a setup for manipulation, betrayal, and deep hurt. My inability to say *no* led to a very difficult and traumatic experience. The lines between professionalism and friendship blurred. My boundaries were pushed, and since they were porous, it wasn't until the line was crossed, I was able to extract myself from the situation and see what had been happening," Dr. Peters explains.

"My firm boundary of saying 'NO' to inappropriate comments and unsubscribing from toxic behavior has allowed me to find peace and harmony in my personal life. Setting boundaries around what I will and will not tolerate in the workplace allowed me to take care of my own well-being. Thanks to Sasha teaching me to set boundaries, I've learned that I am in control of my time. When I am off work, I don't check work e-mails or texts, look at patient charts, or talk to work colleagues. This boundary protects me and allows me to enjoy my family, self-care, friends, and recreation. It is essential for my health that I unplug from work. On the flip side, when I'm at work, I am focused. I get the job done fast and efficiently, so things don't spill over into my time. Also, at work, I speak up against toxicity, negative conversations, and inappropriate behavior because I understand how I can set boundaries," says Dr. Peters.

The truth about being a boundary rebel is that it is not easy. It is hard work, it is difficult, and it requires a persistence that few people understand. You will grow weary at times. You will fail at times to keep your boundaries. That is part of being human; because setting boundaries and sticking to them is so counterculture for women that you will grow weary at times and want to give up. The good news is that there is always space and grace for you to start again. There is no woman out there who is too far gone to learn to set boundaries. You are not too weak to begin again. You are not your worst day, or your biggest mess-up. You can always begin again. Start setting boundaries, no matter how much you have failed to set them in the past.

There is no woman beyond the reach of becoming a boundary rebel.

The reason I know this to be true is because I have watched it firsthand by coaching, teaching women at my conferences, and in my courses where I have taught hundreds of women how to set boundaries. For the last five years, I have watched women pick themselves up, heal their injured souls, and find the courage to set boundaries in their workplaces and homes in order to be well. I have witnessed countless women leave toxic work environments and abusive relationships, and stand up to workplace bullies, stop doing unpaid work, stop doing all the cleaning and cooking and childcare in their homes, hire help, and do it all by embracing their need for radical boundaries. I have seen women with all the different personality types and diverse backgrounds rise from the ashes and become fierce boundary rebels. I have watched countless women say, "No more" to people who consistently take advantage of their lack of boundaries, and instead say yes to themselves. They did it by reminding themselves they are worthy of a life lived well, which begins by doing a boundary inventory and following the steps laid out clearly in this book.

Dr. Andrea Boggild, Associate Professor of Medicine and Infectious Diseases/Tropical Medicine, at the University of Toronto in Canada, is a powerhouse academic leader who teaches, writes, practices medicine full-time, and seems to be able to "do it all." Dr. Boggild took one of my courses on work-life balance in 2021 and learned to set radical boundaries.

"I often liken my existence as an academic physician mother to that of a ship accumulating barnacles as it sails through life. And because scraping barnacles off a ship takes hard work and effort, the path of least resistance is usually to just leave them be and continue doing the tasks that we've accepted," said Dr. Boggild.

"In the fall of 2021, amidst yet another wave of pandemic and furious scrambling to deploy mobile vaccination teams, I was completing the Brave Balance Master Class and reflecting deeply on the words of Dr. Shillcutt. I began to realize that not all those barnacles are created equally, and especially in the case of those who have been affixed to you by a for-profit entity that is benefiting from your free labor. Some are downright parasitic! I examined my calendar and a few roles jumped out where the compensation and recognition (or lack thereof) seriously misaligned with the cognitive effort I was putting forth. That exercise revealed to me what I was losing to do the work, which included time with my family, paid work, and time for personal wellness. Thereafter I flipped the equation and am no longer operating in perpetual crisis mode," she said.

Although it wasn't an easy exercise, Dr. Boggild's ability to set boundaries grew easier, like a muscle you have to injure a bit to grow. "The advice from Dr. Shillcutt that helped me the most was to know the value of an hour of my time. Once I examined my workload (and volunteer-load!) through that lens, it was much easier to draft a list of current tasks and duties to lean out of, and then create an action plan and timeline for offboarding," she explained.

This book is meant to be a guide you can come back to many times in your life, when you feel your work-life control slipping through your fingers. My hope is that when you start to feel overcommitted, exhausted, and careening toward burnout, you will pick-up *Brave Boundaries*, retake the boundary inventory, and reassess. My wish is that instead of beating yourself up for finding yourself in the pit of over-functioning, overpleasing others, and completely drained, that you will deep breathe and regroup.

When I find myself at a space of exhaustion as a high-functioning woman, I simply know it is time to remind myself of a few boundary rebel truths that have become my mantra. I see these truths as a code of conduct. These are truths I know I must remind myself of on a routine basis to resist the need to please others. I want to share these truths with you as we close this journey, and to encourage you to review them, time and time again, when you feel like you are past the point of no-return and just aren't made for this boundary work. When you feel the lowest, the most defeated, *that is when it is most important to have these Boundary Rebel Truths in your view.*

BOUNDARY REBEL TRUTHS

Here are my most important Boundary Rebel Truths. Take a screen shot; save them on your phone. Write them out and put them on your mirror each morning. Save them to your computer home screen. They are life-giving to me, and I hope they become the same for you.

- **Boundary rebels remind themselves often that they are not required to explain their boundaries to anyone.** They know their job is to set their boundaries and move on. They are not afraid of backlash, and they do not apologize for setting radical, lifesaving boundaries. They understand their job is not to make others understand their boundaries, as they cannot control or predict another's response to their boundaries.

- **Boundary rebels constantly create new boundaries and assess the strength of the ones they have.** They routinely repair their fence posts that have become broken around their boundaries and set up new ones. They aren't afraid to step up, step in, and create new boundaries.

- **Boundary rebels recognize that receiving boundary backlash means they are prioritizing their well-being over likeability.** They are not afraid of people's reactions to their boundaries, as they have come to expect a degree of pushback and negative feedback when they set boundaries. They understand that the people who will create the most backlash are likely people who lack boundaries themselves.

- **Boundary rebels understand the difference between approachability and accessibility.** They strive to be approachable; they are not afraid of being approached, because they know that they control their accessibility. They feel free to say *No, thank you,* when the task they are asked to do does not fit in their lives, their desires, or their job descriptions.

- **Boundary rebels crave focus and energy.** They recognize they cannot possess focus without fierce boundaries. They protect their energy by setting and protecting their boundaries.

- **Boundary rebels pick their battles.** They know when to win and when to lay down the battle axe. Boundary rebels know when to retreat back into their boundary, their personal no-fly zone. They protect themselves from the enemy and stay behind the battle lines, especially when they are tired.

- **Boundary rebels accept words for them, not words to them.** They understand that not every word spoken to them is a word *for* them. Boundary rebels protect their hearts and minds by understanding not all criticism or negative interactions have to do with their own actions but may be projection by another individual who is struggling. They allow themselves to accept criticism from people who have their best interests in mind, but they also are able to protect themselves from harsh words that are not meant to improve them or do not come from a place of positive intent.

- **Boundary rebels keep promises to themselves.** Just as they show up for others when they say they will, boundary rebels show up for themselves. They honor themselves by keeping their own words to themselves and prioritize time spent by themselves.

- **Boundary rebels keep showing up, despite setbacks.** They practice self-compassion over self-criticism. Boundary rebels know that showing themselves grace is far more effective for change than beating themselves up and focusing on their past failures and imperfections. Boundary rebels know they will have setbacks and readily give themselves a margin of grace.

One of my superpowers is seeing in women what they may not be able to see in themselves. I love nothing more than empowering women to take actions that align their time with their priorities. Often, when I am asked what I do for a living, I respond with, "I am a cardiac anesthesiologist who teaches women how to have work-life control. I love empowering women." I've grown accustomed to the strange looks. When a colleague at the hospital says, "Hey, I see you on social media. What is *Brave Enough?*" I smile and say, "I teach women how to create boundaries to live empowered."

For years I struggled to verbalize what I do with *Brave Enough,* as I received a lot of backlash for starting a company as a doctor to teach and empower working women. "You should stick to cardiac anesthesia," one of my mentors said. Another mentor told me, "You were well on your way to a path of academic advancement, why are you doing this?" when I shared with him that I started my own company to advance women. It stung. I didn't have a lot of confidence in my early stages when I founded my company. I was afraid of failing. People couldn't grasp why I was starting my own company for women as a successful physician and published clinical researcher. It didn't fit with others' expectations of me. It was difficult for me, and it has taken me several years to know how to respond to people who still don't get me following my passion.

COMFORTABLE BEING UNCOMFORTABLE

I want to share with you a truth that applies to me starting my company and you creating boundaries. You will be scared. You will be uncomfortable. Not everyone will understand or even try to understand why you are making the choices you are. But the truth is this: you have always held the power and freedom to follow your own path. No matter how you were raised, or who has taken your power, or what work or home environment you are in, you have it within you to set boundaries. You have it within you to pivot your way of life and follow your mission. Just as you have the right to change your life mission, you have the right to change how you respond to everyone's expectations of you. You have the right to change your daily routine and prioritize time alone with yourself, just as much as you have the right to change your hair color.

As you have read *Brave Boundaries,* you may have had the defeating thoughts: "It is too late for me," or "I am too much of a people pleaser to set boundaries," but that is simply not true. You have learned a new skill set, and it is up to you to apply it. And I am in your corner, cheering for you. I am not cheering for you because I know you or because I like you, I am cheering for you because I have witnessed countless women apply these concepts, become Boundary Rebels, and find themselves again.

JUST ENOUGH BRAVE

As you step forward, remember this: you are courageous, brave, and ready for any backlash that comes from setting boundaries. You do not have to be a superhero to set boundaries, and you do not always have to be the most courageous person in the room. You just have to be *just enough brave,* brave enough for that day, to set the boundaries you need to be well. Being just enough brave means showing up for yourself in a world that isn't comfortable with women doing so, and saying, *I am choosing my well-being over being liked.*

When you find the courage to choose your well-being over being liked, you are joining good company. You are not alone; you are joining a boundary revolution. Look to your left and to your right. There are boundary rebels everywhere who have your back. The next time you think to yourself, "I cannot do this hard work, I am not strong enough," remember that you are part of a community of women who are applauding you and appreciate you. By setting boundaries, you are inspiring those watching—our daughters, our trainees, and our friends—that it is okay for them to set their own boundaries. You are demonstrating to the next generation of women that it is perfectly acceptable to choose boundaries over pleasing others. Remember the Boundary Rebel truths and go and show others how it is done.

You are a boundary rebel.

RESOURCES

Sasha's Podcast, called **The Brave Enough Show,** can be found on iTunes or wherever you get your podcasts.

Sasha's Community for Professional Women, called **The Table,** is open to enrollment here: https://www.becomebraveenough.com/community

Sasha's annual conference for professional women and women in medicine, Brave Enough, is open here: braveenoughconference.com

Sasha's website, where resources and teachings are available, is found at becomebraveenough.com

Sasha's CME master class, called Brave Balance, which teaches women work-life control through small-group coaching, is found here: https://www.becomebraveenough.com/brave-balance

RECOMMENDED READING

- *Between Grit and Grace: The Art of Being Feminine and For-*
  midable, Sasha K. Shillcutt, Health Communications, Inc.,
  2020.
- *Boundaries: When to Say Yes, How to Say No to Take Control*
  of Your Life, Henry Cloud and John Townsend, Zondervan,
  2017.
- *Breaking Busy: How to Find Peace and Purpose in a World of*
  Crazy, Alli Worthington, Zondervan, 2016.
- *The Confidence Code: The Science and Art of Self-Assurance,*
  Claire Shipman and Katty Kay, Harper Business, 2014.
- *Crucial Conversations: Tools for Talking When the Stakes Are*
  High (Third Edition), Joseph Grenny, Ron McMillan, Al Swit-
  zler, Kerry Patterson, Laura Roppe, McGraw Hill, 2021.
- *A Simplified Life: Tactical Tools for Intentional Living,* Emily
  Ley, Thomas Nelson, 2017
- *Switch: How to Change Things When Change is Hard, Chip*
  Heath and Dan Heath, Broadway Business, 2010

REFERENCES AND BIBLIOGRAPHY

[i]Bernard Baruch, accessed November 12, 2021, https://en.wikiquote. org/wiki/Bernard_Baruch

[ii]Shannon Alder. *The Narcissist Abuse Recovery Bible.* (Springville, UT: Cedar Fort, 2018)

[iii]Dani Matias. NPR Research News. New report says women will soon be majority of college-educated U.S. workers. Accessed November 6, 2021, https://www.npr.org/2019/06/20/734408574/ new-report-says-college-educated-women-will-soon-make-up-majority-of-u-s-labor-f

[iv]Betsey Stevenson and Justin Wolfers. "The paradox of declining female happiness." *American Economic Journal: Economic Policy* 1 (2009): 190–225

[v]Amy Westervelt. *Forget Having It All: How American Messed Up Motherhood and How To Fix It.* (New York, NY: Seal Press, 2018)

[vi]Priscila Rodrigues Armijo, Julie K Silver, Allison R Larson, Philomena Asante, and Sasha Shillcutt. "Citizenship tasks and women physicians: additional woman tax in academic medicine?" *J Women's Health* 30 (2021): 935–943

[vii]Jose E Rodriguez, Maria Harsha Wusu, Tanya Anim, Kari-Claudia Allen, and Judy C Washington. "Abolish the minority woman tax!" *J Women's Health,* 30 (2021): 914–915

[viii]Jess Huang, Irina Starikova, Delia Zanoschi, Alexis Krivkovich, and Lareina Yee. Women in the Workplace McKinsey & Company Report, Sept 2020; accessed November 6, 2021, https://www.mckinsey.com/featured-insights/diversity-and-inclusion/women-in-the-workplace

[ix]Average hours per day parents spent caring for and helping household children as their main activity, American Time Use Survey, US Bureau of Labor Statistics, 2019, accessed November 6, 2021, https://www.bls.gov/charts/american-time-use/activity-by-parent.htm

[x]Arlie Hochschild, *The Second Shift: Working Parents and the Revolution at Home,* first edition (New York, NY: Viking Press, 1989)

[xi]Jolly Shruti, Kent A Griffith, Rochelle DeCastro, Abigail Stewart, Peter Ubel, and Reshma Jagsi. "Gender differences in time spent on parenting and domestic responsibilities by high-achieving young physician-researchers." *Ann Intern Med.* 160 (2014): 344–353.

[xii]Malcom Gladwell. *Outliers: The Story of Success.* (New York, NY: Back Bay Books, 2011)

[xiii]Jerome S. Bruner. *The Culture of Education.* (Cambridge, MA: Harvard University Press, 1996), 136

[xiv]Sasha K. Shillcutt, *Between Grit and Grace*. (Deerfield Beach, FL: Health Communications, Inc., 2020)

[xv]The Bible, New International Version. 1 Corinthians 13:9

[xvi]Dickens, Charles. *Great Expectations*. Wordsworth Classics. (Ware, England: Wordsworth Editions, 1992)

[xvii]Oprah Winfrey, *The Oprah Winfrey Show*, published November 21, 2018. Oprah on the Importance of Setting Boundaries. Accessed November 6, 2021, https://www.youtube.com/watch?v=-OoCSbkQXM4

[xviii]Henry Cloud and John Townsend. *Boundaries in Marriage*. (Grand Rapids, MI: Zondervan, 2002)

[xix]Julie Kashen, Sarah Jane Glynn, and Amanda Novello. How COVID19 sent *Women's Workforce Backwards*. October 30, 2020. accessed November 6, 2021, https://www.americanprogress.org/issues/women/reports/2020/10/30/492582/covid-19-sent-womens-workforce-progress-backward/

[xx]Bureau of Labor Statistics, US Department of Labor, *The Economics Daily*, Women more likely than men to have earned a bachelor's degree by age 29. Accessed *November 06, 2021*, https://www.bls.gov/opub/ted/2016/women-more-likely-than-men-to-have-earned-a-bachelors-degree-by-age-29.htm

[xxi]Ariane Hegewisch and Zohal Barsi. The Gender Wage Gap by Occupation 2019. *The Institute for Women's Policy Research*. Accessed November 6, 2021, https://iwpr.org/iwpr-issues/employment-and-earnings/the-gender-wage-gap-by-occupation-2019/

[xxii]Merriam-Webster Dictionary Online. Accessed November 6, 2021, https://www.merriam-webster.com/dictionary/agency

[xxiii]Melissa J Williams and Larissa Z Tiedens. "The subtle suspension of backlash: A meta-analysis of penalties for women's implicit and explicit dominance behavior." *Psychol Bull.* 142(2016): 165–197

[xxiv]Mara Cadinu, Anne Maass, Alessandra Rosabianca, and Jeff Kiesner. "Why do women underperform under stereotype threat? Evidence for the role of negative thinking." *Psychol Sci.* 16(2005): 572–578

[xxv]Chrstine Logel, Gregory M Walton, Steven J Spencer, Emma C Iserman, William von Hippel, and Amy E Bell. "Interacting with sexist men triggers social identity threat among female engineers." *J Pers Soc Psychol.* 96(2009): 1089–103

[xxvi]The Oracles. Warren Buffet Says the Secret to Success is Saying 'No.' Do You Agree? May 8, 2019, Accessed November 6, 2021. Money, https://money.com/warren-buffett-says-no-to-everything/

[xxvii]T. Hansen, M. It takes guts to say 'no' to your boss, but it's a step on path to excellence. *San Francisco Chronicle* (CA), p. E5. May 20, https://en.wikiquote.org/wiki/Bernard_Baruch2018. Available from NewsBank: Access World News – Historical and Accessed Nov 10, 2021. https://infoweb-newsbank-com.eu1.proxy.openathens.net/apps/news/document-view?p=WORLDNEWS&docref=news/16C051D7744CCF28.

[xxviii]L. Frank Baum. *The Wonderful Wizard of Oz.* (Chicago, IL: George M. Hill Company, 1900)

[xix]Brad Aeon, Aida Faber, and Alexandra Panaccio. Does time management work? A meta-analysis. *PLOS ONE.* 16(2021): e0245066

PERMISSIONS

The following kindly granted me permission to be interview subjects for Brave Boundaries, and I am extremely grateful for their time and stories.

Chapter 1
Dr. Sheritta Strong

Chapter 4
Dr. A
Aimee Lowe, JD

Chapter 5
Dr. D. Bradley
Alli Worthington

Chapter 10
Dr. Cheryl Peters
Dr. Andrea Boggild

ABOUT THE AUTHOR

Sasha Shillcutt, MD, is a tenured professor, gender-equity researcher, award-winning physician, professional coach, and speaker. Her passion is empowering women to be brave enough in their professional and personal lives to set boundaries and gain work-life control. She speaks often at conferences, workshops, and retreats, including her annual conference for women's leadership and well-being. Besides her topics related to her medical practice, she frequently teaches on the topics of career burnout, boundaries, and developing resilient leaders.

Active in social media, she started an online networking group for women physicians that grew to nearly thirteen thousand women internationally. In 2016 she launched her company, Brave Enough, where she leads women through coaching, courses, and conferences to teach them work-life control. Her Brave Enough community and her membership society, The Table, is for women looking to advance in their careers without losing themselves in the process.

Sasha Shillcutt, MD, is a board-certified cardiac anesthesiologist. She received a bachelors' degree in biology from William Jewell College and an MD degree from the University of Nebraska Medical

Center in Omaha, Nebraska. After finishing a residency in anesthesiology, during which she served as chief resident, she completed an executive fellowship in perioperative echocardiography at the University of Utah Medical Center in Salt Lake City. She also holds a Masters in Clinical and Translational Research from the University of Nebraska Medical Center in Omaha, Nebraska. She is a tenured professor of anesthesiology at the University of Nebraska Medical Center in Omaha, Nebraska.

She has published over fifty peer-reviewed scientific articles in professional journals, including the prestigious *New England Journal of Medicine (NEJM,* June 2018) and the *Journal of the American Medical Association (JAMA,* May 2018), and has contributed academic chapters to four books.

In 2016, Sasha was awarded the national American Medical Association's *Women Physicians Inspiring Physician Award* by her peers.

Sasha Shillcutt, MD, taught herself how to be a gritty, grace-filled leader who lives authentically. She wants to help other women be brave enough to do the same. When not writing, speaking, or coaching women, you can find Sasha with her husband, Lance, vacationing near the water or cheering on the side-line of a basketball court or soccer field for one of her four children.

NOTES

NOTES